The Path of Dharma

Buddha's Reflections

A.P. Sharma

*Uncover your own hidden riches by developing wisdom, compassion, nobility and limitless strength by following the Buddhist **Path of Dharma** and discover your veiled and neglected powers to liberate you from your low cravings, and to transcend you to an endless serenity, harmony and freedom.*

Published by

An Imprint of
Pustak Mahal®, Delhi

J-3/16 , Daryaganj, New Delhi-110002
☎ 23276539, 23272783, 23272784 • *Fax:* 011-23260518
E-mail: info@pustakmahal.com • *Website:* www.pustakmahal.com

London Office

51, Severn Crescents, Slough, Berkshire, SL 38 UU, England
E-mail: pustakmahaluk@pustakmahal.com

Sales Centre

10-B, Netaji Subhash Marg, Daryaganj, New Delhi-110002
☎ 23268292, 23268293, 23279900 • *Fax:* 011-23280567

Branch Offices

Bangalore: ☎ 22234025
E-mail: pmblr@sancharnet.in • pustak@sancharnet.in
Mumbai: ☎ 22010941
E-mail: rapidex@bom5.vsnl.net.in
Patna: ☎ 3294193 • *Telefax:* 0612-2302719
E-mail: rapidexptn@rediffmail.com
Hyderabad: *Telefax:* 040-24737290
E-mail: pustakmahalhyd@yahoo.co.in

ISBN 978-81-223-1000-9
Edition : December 2007

Printed at : Param Offsetters, Okhla, New Delhi-110020

Dedicated to

All those who consistently and consciously yearn to cleanse themselves and transcend from their baseness triggered by their daily circumstances.

Acknowledgements

The author thankfully acknowledges the contributions of Shri Eknath Easwaran, Andrew Powell, Nancy Wilson Ross, Shri Yogananda and others who provided him ample of awareness about the Buddhist philosophy and thought-process which helped him to complete this work, primarily for the benefit of the common reader. The noted authors have duly been acknowledged and referred to at the appropriate places in the text.

The author also gratefully acknowledges the generosity of Shri Ram Avtar Gupta, the Managing Director of Pustak Mahal, New Delhi, for awarding this assignment to him. The author thankfully concedes the help and facilities provided to him by his two children, Sanjaya and Vinita, and also by the Brazoria County, Library, in Angleton, Texas, USA. The members of the family and friends, who have directly or indirectly inspired him to complete this work, also deserve his indebtedness.

A.P. Sharma

Contents

Preface

Being in the intimate company of the Buddhist thought-process for more than seven years, I feel I am a convert. I have strongly started feeling that I have ultimately found something for which I had been yearning for so long. Twenty years back when I was working in a Northern University in Nigeria, teaching Educational Philosophy, someone gifted me the book, *Quest of the Quiet Mind*. It contained Jiddu Krishnamurti's philosophical reflections relating 'how to attain human freedom'. His ideas on human freedom greatly fascinated me. As a result, I remained in the whirlpool of his ideology for a good number of years until I assimilated it well. Later on I produced a small work, 'Concept of Freedom' based entirely on Krishnamurti's philosophy of freedom. Similarly, around forty years back a close friend of mine presented me Paramahansa Yogananda's famous book titled *Autobiography of a Yogi*. It almost changed my life and gradually transported me to a different realm that provided me occasional peace of mind. It also inspired me constantly as it helped me to stay with his thought-process for long.

It must have been the year 2003 when I bought the *Dhammapada* from one of the Barns & Nobles bookshops in USA. Initially it was the name of the book which fascinated me, but as I went through it, I felt greatly elated. It contained what I had been longing to seek for so long. Since then I must have gone through it several times. It consists of the material which is not only inspiring but also pragmatic as the ideas contained in it are convincingly acceptable and if desired, can easily be practised too. For example, if you happen to read one of its verses that says, "*Our life is shaped by our minds; we become what we think. Joy follows a pure thought like a shadow that never leaves,*" what would you feel about it? Does it not sound convincing and true? When I look upon the panorama of my own passed life, I feel what Buddha has said is absolutely true. I have led my life completely in line with my beliefs and thoughts only. Therefore, the *Dhammapada* inspired me to write about the unparalleled life of Buddha and to highlight his views on human redemption contained in it.

Although by keeping the company of the sacred thought-process, you may remain in touch with the most desirable notions, but you cannot stay totally unaffected by the mean thoughts which sometimes spring from the lower longings and the feelings of greed, lust, hatred, anger and dislike. Such base thoughts often go on invading us unexpectedly. We often suffer from the complexities created by our conditioning. I have also suffered many a times with certain impelling yearnings that have forced me to go to a low level in thought and action. But merely identifying the base thought-process has often helped me to retrace my lost steps. The parables relating to Buddha's extraordinary life and his reflections projected in the *Dhammapada* are surely a panacea in that respect. It gives us something that we can easily understand and follow. It also helps us to rise above our baseness that restricts us from pursuing the desired path.

The *Dhammapada* is meant for each one of us. It contains 423 verses which are extremely wise reflections of Buddha. The precepts projected through the verses are simple and lucid and can easily be practised and perpetuated. What you require is to keep the company of the Buddhist thought-process and a strong will to pursue it. The Eightfold Path is not difficult to pursue if you have a desire and the will to follow it. Commenting on practising enlightenment Dogen Zenji reflects:

Enlightenment comes from practice,
Thus Enlightenment is limitless;
Practice comes from Enlightenment,
Thus practice has no beginning.

In this humble and small work, I have attempted to present most of Buddha's best ideas projected by him in the *Dhammapada*. I have also narrated the most befitting parables relating to the scene and tried to make the reading more interesting. I very much hope that my attempt in completing this work will benefit all those who want to know more about the Buddhist thought-process and philosophical ideas. However, if some feel that I have missed something of importance and have not come up to their expectations, I beseech their forgiveness for there is no end to go deeper into the realms of knowledge contained in Buddha's parables and the precepts implicit in the *Dhammapada*. The references given in the brackets within the text reflect the serial numbers of the books given in the bibliography. The page numbers are also reflected along with the references.

A.P. Sharma

June 24, 2007

Introduction

The path of *dharma* is always straight if one understands the meaning of the term *dharma* correctly. Most people unthoughtfully love to associate it with traditional beliefs and rituals. It is a kind of conditioning which they love to stick to. Therefore they adore gluing themselves to it without properly considering its meaning. I reckon that the simple meaning of *dharma* is to follow a righteous path which is either prescribed by the tradition or by any recluse, who is not interested in manifesting the self by performing errands to attain his own ends. The path of *dharma* is really simple, away from any meaningless ritualistic traditions, far from holding blind beliefs and sticking to conditioning. It is a way that may lead an individual to a direction which may provide him immense internal bliss. As the individual gradually starts involving with that kind of process by following certain activities that give him solace, comfort and happiness, he begins transcending to a state of mental makeup never known by him before.

In fact, Buddha tried something of that nature and found complete solace in it. In that respect he is one of the few greatest human beings who sincerely tried to help people to get redeemed from the unending misery of life. Buddha did not provide a static composition of belief that one can affirm and be done with it. His teachings are an ongoing path, a *way of perfection*, which one can follow to the highest good. Keeping in view all that he gave us, his life is surely unparalleled. Like a very few others who also worked in that direction to help humans to redeem, he is one of the fewest, who suggests a journey to follow, which can lead us to an endless bliss, as it provides an end to the chain of birth and rebirth, which in Buddha's view is one of the principal causes of human misery.

In fact, Buddha is not the first to start this journey and search for the inner peace. It has been one of the most ancient cherished enterprises of human beings. The search for freedom and tranquillity has inspired a great number of spiritual thinkers from the deepest past to the modern times. In our own times, before the end of the twentieth century, Jiddu Krishnamurti has been another spiritual thinker who tried hard to discover inner peace by de-conditioning our minds. He thought it was primarily on account of conditioning that most human misery was caused. He held strongly that it was through gradual de-conditioning, which required no practice to follow, that one might develop the state of thoughtlessness. He believed that it was a pre-requisite to the state of meditation, which consequently, would lead to attain bliss and inner peace of mind. Much before Krishnamurti, quite a parallel way of thinking was suggested by Buddha. As such, most people who understand Krishnamurti's mind often reckon him as Buddha incarnate. Thus, human mind, since long, has been trying very hard to seek redemption from the day-to-day seduction caused by strong desires, creating apprehensions, fear and delusion. That kind of positive thinking has often crept into the reflective minds of human minds, suggesting that greed, fear, despair, hatred and other things of that nature are not the true states of right thinking.

An ancient Indian book, *Dasabhumika-isvara*, presents a vivid account of those mental afflictions imposing humanity that have continued producing fear, strife, plunder, hatred, lust and all what we consider harmful and undesirable for human mind. It says:

> *Because of continually slipping into*
> *erroneous views, because of ignorance,*
> *because of pride, because of mental*
> *fixation of desires pushed by cravings,*
> *because of deceit and falsehood, because*
> *of deeds connected with envy and jealousy*
> *because of actions leading to delusion,*
> *because of seeds in the mind, intellect, and*
> *consciousness bound to flows of lust,*
> *existence, and ignorance.*

Perhaps on account of a sustained desire to attain freedom from turmoil and innumerable apprehensions, human mind has tried hard to discover a number of systems of thought and action from the ancient times. It has given birth to a variety of new systems of thought-processes, which have sometimes suggested measures that include denial to leading even an ordinary way of life. Many ancient Hindu recluses followed that path to discover the inner peace of mind. In the beginning, Buddha also tried very hard to attain the peace of mind by refusing to eat and to provide any comforts to his body for a good number of days. It gradually resulted in weakening of his body leading almost to decay. If he had not restored it by accepting some nourishment a little before its decay, he would have gone without contributing anything to the humanity. Thus, for centuries, numberless ways were tested to attain the inner peace of mind. In that connection, a vast literature was also produced and was passed on to the posterity orally for centuries. But later on written material developed out of the oral transmissions.

The *Dhammapada* is one of the finest examples of that kind. It was initially communicated orally then created in written form. *Dhammapada* simply means 'statement of principles or precepts'. It is a popular collection of maxims that gradually lead one to the path of inner peace. Most of the discourse contained in it is accredited to Gautama Buddha, who came to this earth almost five hundred years before Christ. No one is wholly definite when it exactly began, but most historians hold that the man, who created it, was known as Buddha. He was born approximately in 563 BC at a place known as Lumbini, a village in southern Nepal, quite close to the Indian border. Gautama lived for eighty years. When he died in 483 BC, Pericles was forty-seven and Socrates only six years old. "The future Buddha was given the personal name Siddhartha in addition to his clan name Gautama. His father was the leader of the people known as the Shakyas and so Buddha is also frequently referred to as Shakyamuni or 'Sage of the Shakyas'. The title 'Buddha' itself is an honorific word, meaning 'The Awakened One'. (9: p.13)

Lest the reader should develop any confusion, it is therefore necessary, at this juncture, to clarify that Prince Siddhartha, Shakyamuni, Gautama Buddha and Buddha are all the same person. Gautama is believed to have attained perfect peace of mind after a dogged struggle for years in its quest. He then spent almost forty-five years travelling from place to place, preaching others the way to attain the internal peace and freedom which was required to attain *nirvana* or self-realisation. Buddha addressed forest ascetics, nobles, priests and village people in the language and culture that were common during his times. He neither accepted the authority of tradition, nor preached any novel views prevalent in the new age. He did not teach any dogmas that could lead to freedom and enlightenment.

He condemned the ancient caste system for he considered it to have become oppressive. He totally rejected the ritualism created by the old priesthood. He talked to the people from all walks of life in locally prevalent language. He was so lucid and confident in preaching and procedure that most of the yogis and ascetics left their own systems of pursuance and entered Buddhist discipline. All that happened because Buddha possessed great clarity, perfect calmness and was an awakened person.

The oral tradition containing Buddha's precepts was finally written down in Pali language, which was a newly developed literary language. It was based on regularisation of the vernaculars used by Buddha and his disciples. A great number of discourses between Buddha and his disciples in the oral tradition demonstrate deep calmness and unchangeable status of his religion. Buddha focused his teachings leading to purification of the self, strength of character and final attainment of freedom. Buddhism in totality refers to the process of individual liberation from misery and ignite hope to attain perfect peace of mind. This is what has been contained in the *Dhammapada* relating to Buddha's teachings. 'The attainment of perfect peace is referred to as the Lesser Journey while its goal to reach *nirvana* is called the Magic City. From there, a new viewpoint opens up. It is known as the Great Journey whose goal of enlightened knowledge and vision is called the Land of Treasures. Once in that realm of consciousness, the ultimate journey is revealed, this is called the Tantra or Fundamental Continuity, wherein heaven and earth are united.'(3: p.5)

Thus, Buddha directed his followers to travel step-by-step in the quest of perfection and attainment of total tranquillity. He believed that the final achievement of the journey towards the attainment of *nirvana* depended on the insight, peace and self-control acquired in the course of the Lesser Journey.

Only those who religiously (sincerely) attempted to acquire a right insight, serenity and forbearance during their Lesser Journey, were able to advance further on the road to *nirvana.* But those who attempted to commence the Greater Journey without the attainment of the spiritual provisions to be acquired during the Lesser Journey and those who did not take that Journey seriously at any stage, were not able to reach their destination.

When Buddha initially started stressing the importance of completing the Lesser Journey strictly as its role was very crucial before attempting to start the Greater Journey, a great number of people who believed they had already reached self-realisation, left his assembly. According to one of the scriptures, the *Sadharmapundarika-sutra*, the people who left the assembly were those who had already travelled the Lesser Journey solemnly and believed to have attained some sort of serenity and peace of mind. Much of this kind is also recorded in the books of history of those times. It reveals that there have been groups of followers who did not accept Buddha's teachings to travel on to the road to Greater Journey for they believed they had already attained *nirvana* by following the Lesser Journey. Such ascetics remained attached to their own beliefs and self-styled *nirvana.* Most of the followers, who did not adhere to Buddha's advice to go beyond the Lesser Journey, were those who took the Lesser Journey as the final stage of *nirvana.* They held that there was no need to track through any kind of journey after that.

The Dhammapada

The *Dhammapada* is one of the oldest and most revered classics of the Buddhist faith. It is primarily drawn from the ancient Pali Tenet, which consists of one of the great bodies of primary Buddhist literature. The original text consists of four hundred and twenty-three sayings grouped into twenty-six chapters. The *Dhammapada* is well known for its simplicity and lucid readability. It is haply the best basic on Buddhism to be discovered anywhere else. The *Dhammapada* provides a map for the road to reach the highest good. **We can start this journey whenever we like. As we advance on this road and make progress, the scenery of our values, objectives and understanding of life around us changes gradually.** The verses contained in the *Dhammapada* can be taken and appreciated as prudent philosophical reflections, but all what is contained in it is one of the best literatures found in the whole world.

In fact, the *Dhammapada* is a definite guide to attain the highest goal life can offer to anyone. It is the goal of self-realisation. Eknath Easwaran holds that 'if everything else were lost, we would need nothing more than the *Dhammapada* to follow the way of Buddha... The *Dhammapada* does not actually contain stories or parables or any instructions that distinguish the main Buddhist sutras or scriptures. It is simply a collection of practical verses, perhaps collected from direct disciples who desired to conserve what they had heard from Buddha himself. It has Buddha's teachings — his intellectual reflections, compressed in a theme — anger, greed, fear, joy, pleasure, happiness, impurities.'(4: p.7) But this collection of verses does not seem to be a scattered collection. When we read it, it seems to be a single whole harmoniously composed and connected. It suggests as if all what was told, took place in the presence of the great Master, Buddha. All those who can sincerely follow it to the end, can reach the highest goal of life — self-realisation. Thus, it proposes a great promise to each one of us to reach the most desired goal in life.

It is so disheartening that the faith which started from India has almost disappeared from this land except that its small vintages still lurk here and there. But the most outstanding evidence that Buddhism continues to be an unlimited source of inspiration, is the charm it now holds for most of the Western world. To a great number of people in America and Europe, Buddhism seems to be a religion or tradition well-suited to them and to the future of the entire mankind because it is based on reason and not on blind faith. It also equates to the scientific spirit as it leads to a convincing acceptance being much akin to the truth.

The Existing Environment

At the time of the birth of Siddhartha during the middle of the sixth century, the Indian civilisation was almost ancient for it was fully flourished. The Aryan tribes, migrated from Central Asia, herded in groups, wandered from place to place in the early stages of their resettlement. Gradually they entered through the Indus River gates into the Indian subcontinent. When these tribes came to India, they found a flourished civilisation which had been there for more than a thousand years. It had its own established features of the Hindu faith which consisted of practising meditation, and worship of Lord Shiva as God. Along with Shiva, the Divine Mother or Kali was also the attention of their worship.

The social order which the Aryans had brought with them was different from the existing Indian social climate. It consisted of an elite class of people, known as Brahmins, who were primarily priests. These priests were dedicated to remember hymns and perform rituals, also related to the other lands from where the Aryans had come to India. To absorb all what is different and foreign, is perhaps, one of the Indians' special traits. Therefore, Indians gradually absorbed and assimilated the new religion without much inconsistency. Consequently, even in the earliest of the Indian scriptures, such as the *Rig Veda*, we find Aryans' nature-gods well integrated and accepted. The ascetics and the ancient Indian wise people considered 'Truth is one'. Thus, a different idea, such as there was also a nature-god, was easily accepted and absorbed in the Indian culture.

When Siddhartha was born, two sub-currents of faith were prevalent in the Indian subcontinent. One was followed by the majority of the people consisted of the social and religious order. They had complete faith in the Vedas. The Brahmins were totally in charge of it, protecting the ancient scriptures and responsible for performing the rituals. The people belonging to the other group followed a tradition, which was comparatively ancient than the already defined one. This group loved performing activities beyond rituals and accepted most of the practices cultivated by the Brahmin priests. They strongly believed that by practising spiritual discipline, a divine life could be realised.

Vedic tradition clearly approves that man's first highest obligation is to perform all the necessary social obligations and then to retire to a lonely place or an *ashram* preferably in the Himalayas or forests and learn from a learned teacher how to conceive God. This kind of choice has often been misconceived by the ancients and many a times also by the modern ascetics who desire to realise God by torturing their mind and body to obtain freedom or to know the truth. But the truth is that the sort of asceticism in which the body is tortured, has hardly been popular either in the ancient or modern times in India. The great Buddha also discovered it gradually before his enlightenment that torturing the body would not lead him on to the road of self-realisation.

An *ashram* was mostly considered a kind of retreat where the seeker would live with a teacher, as part of his family. He would lead him to follow a life of simplicity in order to focus on the inner growth, broaden the understanding and constantly keep the aim of self-realisation in mind. These men and women desirous to learn the highest good, sometimes graduated from one of the forest academies, going on to become a teacher. It was also quite likely that the seeker would return to the society, well-disciplined and trained in body and mind, contribute to the people in some form to enlighten them in their day-to-day life. Such cultivated and disciplined persons need not to run away from life but to control it and master the passions that distract them to follow the right path. Thus, what the ancient sages taught the seekers was to live with their people, and help them bring change as much as possible. In the modern times, good examples of that kind could be of Swami Vivekananda and Paramahansa Yogananda who actually lived with their teachers for years and learnt the process of enlightenment.

In fact, what the early Vedic sages taught us was not different from what Buddha said initially. These sages provided ideas which Buddha voiced later on. The sages taught that self-realisation simply meant good health, vitality, long life and a happy balance of inward and outward activity of the self. They also suggested that human destiny ultimately lies in our own hands provided we are able to master the passions of the mind:

> *We are what our deep, driving desire is. As our deep, driving desire is, so is our will. As our will is, so is our deed. As our deed is, so is our destiny.*
> (Brihadaranyaka iv.4.5)

The sages insisted on ***knowing***, and not simply learning of facts. They insisted that a direct experience of truth was more important than simply learning. It was neither difficult, nor it could be taken as quite a scholarly achievement. They strongly held that knowledge meant realisation, which meant understanding and comprehension. If one wants to know the truth, one must make it real, must live it out in mind, word and action. Everything else of value follows from that only. But to achieve it correctly, one would also require following some method without which its attainment would not be feasible. The method these sages suggested to pursue the truth, they called *brahmavidya*. It meant to focus one's attention closely on the contents of consciousness. In simple words, it meant 'meditation' only.

The modern thinkers and the scientists reckon 'meditation' as scientific because it leads to right reflections, which ultimately make one reach the truth. But the point of view of the sages in that respect was different. They thought it to be the search for truth, which under all the conditions was unchangeable. The sages of the Vedic times were far more pragmatic in their outlook and approach towards knowing. They looked not at the world outside, but at the human knowledge inside. They required to know the unchangeable truth only and discarded everything which was not permanent. Like the sensations of a dream are not real when one awakens, they condemned all what they could not experience in reality. They tried hard to peel out personality layer by layer and found nothing permanent in the mass of perceptions, emotions, drives and thoughts, and what we call 'I'. But they found that after removing everything, an intense awareness remained which they called consciousness. This they called *atman*, the ultimate ground of human personality, or 'the Self'.

Dharma as a Universal Standard

From the time of *Rig Veda* and onwards, scriptures in India came forward with certainty that 'there is an order in the entire creation, which is reflected in each part of the creation'. Thus, during the Vedic times in India it was conceived that 'the natural world is not composed of physical material but it also consists of human action and thought, and all that is uniformly governed by universal law. It is the law which is called *dharma* in Sanskrit. The term comes from *dhir* which means to hold or to bear, and its root sense is the essence of a thing, the defining quality that holds it together as what it is.'(4: p.12) In a wider sense, the meaning of the term *dharma* is to be consistent with the central law of life. It means all things and events are part of an inseparable whole. But its meaning is far wider and needs great attention to comprehend. Perhaps it is one of the richest words in meaning. In the sphere of human activity, it indicates human behaviour in line with the unity. At times, it indicates righteousness. Sometimes it expresses justice, duty or one's obligations towards religion or society. It also connotes that one who strictly follows the truth is a true follower of *dharma* and also a true human being. In other words, it means practising loyalty, nobility, and to cultivate forgiveness, kindness, truthfulness and compassion. 'Buddhism states that any teaching that genuinely helps people to develop should be considered to be *dharma*. *Dharma* is a blueprint for the unfolding of the full potential of human consciousness. It is a clearly laid-out path of development by means of which one can grow beyond one's accidental conditioning and wake up to understand the true nature of reality.' (19: p.3) The essence of *dharma* in the ancient India was to do no harm to any living being. Thus, the meaning of *dharma* was almost all pervasive.

The ancient sages held that nothing happened in this world by chance. The events are also not predestined but they happen as everything has a cause which leads to an effect. Human thoughts and ideas are also included in this respect. Thoughts give birth to other thoughts. They cause things to happen. Therefore, what we think has significance, and has consequence for us and the world around us. Our thinking conditions us and impels us to act in the way we think. In that respect, all the results or events that take place affecting others and ourselves, are our own responsibility. A good example has been presented by Eknath Easwaran in this respect, "Someone who is always angry is bound to provoke anger in others." Such examples indicate the law of *karma*, reflected in Hinduism and Buddhism. *Karma* means some activity or an act, done as a cause or consequence or effect. Therefore, actions in accord or harmony with *dharma* bring good *karma* and selfish actions always lead to accumulate unfavourable *karma* and cause pain and inflict sorrow.

Besides this kind of founded belief in the law of *karma*, there was another important thought rampant with the ancient sages. It was that we ourselves are responsible to receive rewards or punishments in line with our actions that accumulate *karma*. There was no heavenly agency to punish or reward us. It was not regarded as a precept of religion but as a law of nature. 'As you sow, so shall you reap,' was repeatedly reflected by Jesus too. The Vedic sages also held that *karmic* debts and our unfulfilled desires do not disappear even when we die. Our strong desires (ego) remain in the universe to give birth to life at the time of conception when the right moments arrive. Thus, our ancient sages found out the way describing human personality and the goal of life. The only goal of life, for them, could be *moksha* which was the state of complete freedom from the ego or freedom from delusion. They described it a state in which the self is totally integrated with consciousness. That was the only state of human liberation or freedom. Jiddu Krishnamurti also suggests a similar kind of freedom by detaching oneself from the rampant conditioning and persistent ego. Buddha called it *nirvana,* which meant extinction of the sense of a separate ego.

With that sort of social and religious environment rampant during the time of the birth of Siddharatha, it was rather out of question for him not to be influenced by the prevailing circumstances. The ideas of *karma* and transmigration (rebirth) were not merely philosophical reflections of the sages, but realities which people considered to be true and personal. All looked towards *dharma* as a universal standard which they obeyed and adopted. It was, therefore, quite natural that Buddha made some of those ideals as his own and cultivated and propagated them too later on.

CHAPTER ONE

Birth of the Enlightened

The sixth century BC was a time of cultural expansion in Europe and Asia. During Buddha's times more than two dozens kingdoms lay along the banks of the river Ganges. These states were also the centres where India's ancient scientific traditions started to grow. At birth, he was given the name Siddhartha. The name Siddhartha has a connotation, which means 'one who has attained the purpose in life'. As his father Shuddodhana was a king, Siddhartha's upbringing was highly comfortable. Once while conversing to his disciples he reflected to them about his childhood days: "I was delicate, O monks, excessively delicate. I wore garments of silk and my attendants held white umbrella over me. My unguents were always from Benaras."(15: p. 4)

Siddhartha was greatly a gifted child. It is told that he received excellent education befitting to become a successful king in future. He was outstanding in sports, highly skilful in archery and different physical games that required extraordinary courage and strength. He was amazingly handsome and possessed a very attractive physique. He had a swift and intensified intellect implicit with reflective thinking and compassionate nature. At the age of sixteen he was married to Yashodhara a beautiful princess from one of the neighbouring states. Within a couple of years of their marriage, Yashodhara gave birth to a male child who was named Rahul by his grandparents. Siddhartha was a lucky person who possessed everything from his childhood. He had a noble descent and an attractive personality. These were rare gifts from the gods. Ordinarily only a few get such endowments in this world. He appeared stately and owned elephants and every kind of wealth that a person could long for on this earth.

Historians depict that an astrologer had already predicted at Siddhartha's birth that the configuration of the stars at that time was such, which indicated that the child would either be one of the greatest kings of India or renounce the world in quest of truth and be a world redeemer. His father did not want him to leave the household. As such every kind of arrangement for his pleasure and amusement was made from his early childhood. Three palaces and thousands of dancing girls were placed at his disposal. Strict orders were given that the prince should not be exposed to ugliness or displeasures. But despite all such amenities and godly gifts, like a handsome appearance and an extraordinarily beautiful wife, a kind of discontentment dawned upon him when he entered his twenties. Legends display that the main reason of that sort of unhappiness is assigned to four different kinds of sights that changed the entire scenario of his life.

Four Different Sights

In spite of king's strict orders that the prince must not be exposed to any doleful sights, he could not stop the destined. One day, a feeble old man who had broken teeth, grey hair, crooked and bent body, and was walking with the help of a staff, encountered him all of a sudden while he was heading on a joyride. That day he learnt that 'man also gets older and becomes weak'. Another day he met a man who was diseased and was lying on the roadside. The third time he saw a dead body carried by some people on their shoulders.

Finally he was encountered by a head-shaven monk with a bowl in his hand bearing a saffron robe. On enquiring, his charioteer, Channa, told him that the monk had withdrawn from the world in search of liberation. These sights filled him with great remorse and a strong feeling of sadness pervaded him, providing him thoughts relating to renouncing this world. 'In increasing anxiety, Siddhartha began to ask himself how it is possible for anyone truly to enjoy living, feel happy, experience lasting pleasure, when finally, for everyone, without exception, there is no escape from suffering, sadness, loss and, at the end, inevitable personal extinction. Why should a man wish to be born at all; for that matter, why should anyone even wish to give birth?'(12: p.6) Did life have a purpose or was it simply a show of passing events? Such unusual questions started invading his mind. Gradually he came to conclude that everything was bound to change. The moment that thought crept into his mind, he became extremely restless. More questions of that nature started bothering him constantly.

As the anxiety to know the answers of those questions grew in him increasingly, he tried hard to know their answers from the wise courtiers. But within the palace none was able to satisfy him. When he encountered the fourth sign, the wandering holy man, he got a new direction and probably it gave him some sort of answer to his agonising questions. Like the wandering mendicant, bearing simple clothing, with a bowl in his hands, he should also leave the palace and go forth to discover right answers to his questions. But it was not that easy to leave the place of his birth as by now he had a beautiful wife and a son whom he loved so much. The ties and bonds of love they had created were far more difficult to break. Yet there was no choice for him as he knew that he must soon leave the life for ever which looked so fascinating. So one night after taking a long look at both Yashodhara and Rahul, who were sleeping unaware of his decision, he stole outside the palace. When he left only his faithful companion, Channa, was with him. Siddhartha was quite young at that age to follow the path of a recluse. By then, he was hardly twenty-nine years old. Such withdrawals were customarily prescribed for the Indians by the tradition after their middle age was gone. But Siddhartha's early education and his understanding of the terms *karma* and *nirvana* must have provided him such ideas. Therefore, he decided to leave home much earlier to conquer his *karma* in order to get the final release from this world.

It was still dark, a little before dawn when his trusted companion, Channa, brought him his horse. Both travelled towards the east until the light of the Sun was visible. When they reached the bank of the river Anoma, Siddhartha came down from his horse. The prince then removed his ornaments and the robes, handed them to Channa, and asked him to take them back to the palace. Channa, who had been the prince's sole companion for years, could not bear him go as a recluse. With tears in his eyes, he earnestly pleaded to go with him. But Siddhartha did not agree to his requests and implored him to leave.

Then the prince put on a simple robe, cut off his black hair, took a bowl in his hand and plunged into the world to find answers to the troubling questions. As he tracked through the forests, he discovered some renowned teachers whom he already knew well. He stayed with them for some time, studied yoga and practised meditation. But the questions that led him to leave his palace still remained unanswered. He then tracked on his own to discover some convincing answers to those difficult questions.

Siddhartha wandered in the forests for six long years. He forced himself to bear all kinds of penances. He thought that starvation and lack of sleep would give him the insight to discover right answers to the questions that had been disturbing him for so long. As the intake of food reduced to one grain of rice a day, his body became extremely weak. Now he was unable to meditate or to perform the routine duties on account of extreme weakness of his body. It was at that time that Sujata, the daughter of a nearby householder brought him some rice puddings in offering. He accepted it and ate slowly to satisfy his hunger. He suddenly got an insight at that time that starving the body would not provide him the required answers to his quest. It was then that he learnt that starvation could not break his identification with the body. Then with a redoubled determination, he sat down to meditate until he discovered the right answer. Near Gaya, a town in Bihar, he found a serene place under a Bo Tree where he sat down to meditate. As he drew himself straight for meditation, he took a vow that he would not get up from there until he found a way beyond decay and death.

Determined and completely implicit in peace, he passed into deep meditation. When his senses closed down and concentration grew undisturbed by the awareness of the outside world, Mara (Death) approached him to tempt. Legends depict that first Mara sent his three most beautiful daughters. He requested Siddhartha Gautama to have any of them. But Siddhartha did not pay any heed to Mara's invitation. He continued plunging into deeper concentration which was beyond temptation of any extraordinary beauty of mortal women. Then Mara tried to disturb his meditation by pressing into his thoughts avalanche of passions pervaded with lust, doubt, hypocrisy, desire for honour and fame. But Siddhartha continued sinking into deep concentration. Undisturbed by the thoughts of the outside world, beyond the reach of Mara, Siddhartha Gautama had now reached the final stage of his attainment. The distinction of a separate personality totally ceased as he entered into the profound stillness in which thought stops. In that state of final attainment, he remained throughout that night. When it was dawn the tree under which he had meditated whole night, abruptly bloomed. He was now enlightened. He was no more Siddhartha Gautama, but had changed to be known as Buddha, which simply meant the Enlightened One.

When Mara felt that he was defeated, he asked his armies of temptation to withdraw. Mara was now depressed for his task of diverting Siddhartha from the right path remained unfulfilled. In his final depression, Mara asked Buddha how he would be able to help others whose hearts and minds were full of selfish desires, although he had reached *nirvana*. Mara continued his query and asked him further that how many people would listen to him and strive like him to reach the stage he had attained after years of hard toil, discipline and determination. Buddha did not possess any immediate answer to those questions. Without replying him any more, he once again plunged into a deep concentration. When he realised that he had a right answer to Mara's unprecedented query, slowly he opened his eyes and told him: "Perhaps, there will be a few who will listen... To those who will listen, I will teach *dharma*, and for those who follow it, the *dharma* itself will set them free." Listening to Buddha's answer, Mara was finally unarmed and departed at once totally defeated.

Thus, free from Mara's evil spells, fully enlightened, possessing an unending serenity, endowed with a deep insight and a highly reflective vision, Siddhartha was now a changed person. The long sought awakening dawned on him. The Bo Tree under which he was seated with an unbending determination, in Buddhist history, is known and worshipped to this day as a sacred Indian site at Bodh Gaya. It is the tree, in view of the Buddhists, that a greatest event in all human history took place on a full moon night in the month of May in 544 BC. Some historians hold a later date of his enlightenment. In Japan, the Buddhists believe that he was enlightened some time in December. Perhaps it is not the date that matters much to the Asian or Indian thinkers. For them, it is the process of enlightenment and the enlightenment itself which carries Buddha's message that matters most.

A Unique Experience

What is that enlightenment? Can it be explained in words? Perhaps it is difficult to do so. The man who is awakened is in no doubt about its occurrence for he has experienced it clearly. Probably he may not describe it very accurately, but he knows what has happened to him during that experience. He knows all that as he has really experienced it. Particular emotional and physical states of mind and body can hardly be explained at times. Even aesthetic questions and expressions are difficult to be answered so easily. When Socrates once asked the potter, named Mouse, 'which of the pots was beautiful in his shop', the potter started scratching his head for he did not know its exact answer. After a while, the potter indicated towards one pot and said that that particular pot was beautiful. Socrates went ahead and asked him another question, "What is this thing called beautiful, Mouse?" "Beautiful?" said Mouse, and looked puzzled for a minute, and touched the shoulder of the pot he had been making. Then he said, "I don't know about the beautiful, Socrates. I only know about good pots. A good pot is a beautiful pot to me."

"But why is it good, Mouse?" Socrates asked him.

Then pointing towards a pitcher, Mouse said, "That is a good pitcher. It is good for something... In fact to my way of thinking, unless it does the thing that it is supposed to do it, can hardly be called a pitcher at all."

Socrates uttered slowly, "Then it must be the goodness in things that makes them beautiful and useful...." (8: p.9-10)

Probably Mouse did not know how to define exactly the term 'beautiful'. But he knew it well that something which was considered beautiful was good and useful too. Like Mouse who understood the meaning of beautiful well but was unable to define it, Buddha also understood the meaning of enlightenment as he had experienced it, but haply he too was unable to put it in words before his first five disciples as it was really difficult for him to do so.

The experience he underwent during his enlightenment provided him an unusual understanding about the metaphysical matters, related to the nature of the self and its relationship with the universe. It provided him awareness to transcend above the rampant customary ideology that promised to attain freedom. Consequently he condemned the practices and the ritualistic traditions the Brahmins used to propagate at that time. They merely taught the people for their own benefits. As a pragmatist, Buddha believed in putting the horse before the cart and driving it hard. Perhaps he was not able to explain clearly in words the meaning of enlightenment. But he had conceived it correctly. It helped him possess an aim which he followed most doggedly until he left this world. Without worrying for things that had no relationship with the good, he continued his journey to help people to attain liberation. Perhaps this must have caused him to create the first verse in the *Dhammapada*, which says,

"We are what we think." Therefore, he always emphasised on cultivating right kind of thought-process and advised people to follow it religiously. In his opinion, only a wise person was capable of following the right path. No side tracks would be helpful in the attainment of happiness and liberation. While reflecting on the theme, 'The Awakened' in the *Dhammapada*, he said, "Stay away from all kinds of evil, cultivate the good, cleanse your mind;" this sums up the teaching of Buddha.' Such a clear thinking certainly helped him. As a result, he always condemned side tracks and the practice of traditional rituals that carried people nowhere.

At this point, I recall a parable relating to one of the disciples of Buddha, named Malunkyaputta. He once came in an agitated mood to ask him answers to certain questions that had been disturbing him for long. The disciple told him, "I have certain questions, which if you don't reply, I shall leave the Order." After listening to what the disciple had said, Buddha looked at him and replied very calmly. He told him that if he wanted to leave the *sangha*, he could do so for he never asked him to join the Order; he came to join it with his own desire. Listening to it the disciple calmed down. Then Buddha asked him, "Tell me, what your questions are." The disciple told him that he wanted to know whether heaven and hell existed, and whether there was any soul. Listening to his questions, Buddha smiled and said to him, "You are behaving like the person who has been shot by a poisonous arrow and is grievously wounded, but is not permitting the physician to take the arrow out from his body before he learns who shot at him and what was his cast or religion. By the time all that could be known the wounded man would surely die." When the disciple heard the reply, he left totally satisfied.

What Buddha meant by it was that one must direct one's total efforts towards the goal and not towards the direction that would lead him nowhere. It was the right procedure and earnestness towards the goal that would help one to attain *nirvana*. In fact, what he was reflecting to Malunkyaputta was his own experience that led him to attain *nirvana*. As soon as Buddha attained *nirvana*, the perspectives of his life were totally changed. He himself was in no doubt about his particular physical or emotional conditions. By keeping a constant spiritual discipline, intensive meditation and right reflections, he had experienced enlightenment through his intuitive faculties. It was the condition through which he completely realised that his own self and the universe were one and not separate entities at all. It also provided him the thought that everything was connected and related, and therefore, there was always a cause for things to happen which certainly led to create effects. But in that kind of realisation, Buddha did not conceive any divine intervention to make it happen as was believed customarily. It was a finding that Buddha had made through his own determined and continued efforts. He had found the way to lead man to the state of perfect tranquillity by controlling his own mind and senses.

During the state of his being enlightened, Buddha conceived that his entire life was in an ever-moving process of becoming and destruction. Within that constantly moving process of becoming and non-becoming, he clearly discovered that it was his own illusion or ego that led to further continuity of existence. In simple words, 'it is man's ego or unlimited desires that go on binding him to reincarnate or to take another birth after the final demise happens. The idea of human existence, therefore, is simply a delusion created by one's ego.' Buddha, therefore, conceived the 'self' as a compound of different kinds of psychological reactions and responses caused by one's ego with no fixed centre.

As soon as Buddha understood this fact about life, it provided him a complete sense of freedom that delivered him from all sorts of ego ignited by greed, feelings of attachment and hatred, and desire and non-reality. In that sort of realisation, he experienced such a kind of joy that he had never known before. It was a unique kind of serenity which led him through the states of bliss and infinite knowledge with which he could see what an ordinary human eye was unable to experience. He was an enlightened being now. Perhaps it was that joy and the state of liberation after his enlightenment which inspired him to express the total truth about the possibility of human liberation in the verses contained in the *Dhammapada*. It is a collection of more than four hundred verses translated from Pali that contain 'how one's right mental and physical conduct can lead to liberation'.

There are numerous descriptions regarding the length of time and different kinds of experiences Buddha had when he attained the enlightenment. Some stories relate how he conceived the vision of all his former lives and some tell how he could foresee the essentials contained in his future teachings. During his later teachings, Buddha disclosed to his disciples several times that in the state of enlightenment he clearly saw that 'the entire universe was integrated with an ongoing process of a system composed of different kinds of life, passing ceaselessly from one form to another, without stopping the flow of energies and appearances'. (12: p.17) That sort of Buddha's finding was extremely revolutionary because the rampant view of liberation during his times held a strong belief in the existence of a supernatural power that was all-pervading. Buddha discovered something different from that. He discovered the truth that was totally against the popular conceptions rampant at that time. The truth he found out also did not contain any blind faith in the process of its discovery. What he had discovered was the truth which was not only conceivable by reasoning but could also be experienced personally. The path that he had discovered required unceasing personal efforts that demanded determination and hope to attain it. Buddha after the attainment of his enlightenment could stay in that state of bliss for ever if he liked for his own purpose of life had been fulfilled. But he possessed an unending compassion for all human beings. As such, he decided to stay on this earth among humans to deliver them from misery and agony and convey his message to them to help them attain freedom.

I am reminded at this juncture of Jiddu Krishnamurti, the philosopher saint of late twentieth century, who too after the attainment of a similar state of liberation, relinquished all the worldly attachments. He not only dissolved the Assembly of the Star of the East of which he was appointed head by the Theosophical Society, he also told the assembled people not to ever worship him as a guru for he feared that it would lead them to cultivate conditioning which could restrict them to attain liberation. (13: p.42)

Legends say that after his complete liberation, Buddha stayed at that spot for a few more weeks before leaving Gaya. During this period, he submerged in *nirvana* several times and went deeper into the nature of happiness and misery. Then he went out to line up with his teaching. He tracked the dusty roads and paths of India for nearly fifty years. Now he was about to enter his eightieth year of life. His hair grew white and body infirm. But with hard toil which proved highly productive and fruitful, he continued spreading his message to the people. His untiring spirit helped him to preach his ego-shattering and redeeming messages to the multitude of people. Finally he was able to establish an Order of monks and nuns that challenged the existing corrupt practices propounded by the priests and the Brahmins of that time. His teachings provoked a direction of new thinking among the people. It ignited in them a new wave of thinking that challenged the innumerable meaningless ritualistic practices prevalent in the society on account of Hindu priests' supremacy and consistent advocacy.

The twelfth century Mahabodhi Temple at Bodh Gaya, the site of Buddha's Enlightenment and the holiest Shrine of the Buddhist world

Besides training monks and supervising affairs of his Order, Buddha maintained a ceaseless schedule of meeting the public. He preached, counselled and comforted the troubled and distressed. He encouraged the faithful and the sincere, who loved his Order and followed the *dharma*. People came to him right across the country from distant lands. They asked questions and clarified their uncertainties that had engulfed their lives with doubt and darkness for long. He welcomed everyone whole-heartedly and provided them comfort with words and kind demeanour which they had never known so far. He had a unique way of preaching. It enabled people to stand against the existing atrocities. Gradually they learnt to reject the prevalent practices. It helped them acquire peace of mind and serenity they had never known in their lives.

Buddha had an extraordinary way of routine of his life. It was implicit with a method of retreat and return which is perhaps the core of most of the creativity. He withdrew for six years then came back for forty-five years. His each year was divided similarly. He remained for nine months in the world, meeting all the people who came from far and wide to see him. It followed by a three months' retreat in the rainy season. During this period, he stayed with his monks advising and preaching them the ways and methods to practise *dharma* and to maintain the Order. His daily routine was similarly patterned. He returned to his hermitage three times in a day but his public hours were pretty long. Perhaps during his retreat, he often meditated to find answers to certain difficult questions and to find ways to redeem the needy and the desirous. This is how he devoted his life for the good of the people.

CHAPTER TWO

The Basic Concepts

When Buddha left Gaya and started wandering in the northern part of Indian states, he stayed occasionally at some place for a brief recess and to deliver his message to all those who gathered around him. While having entered the realms of enlightenment a number of times on the night when he first experienced it, he had drawn plans in his mind to travel through the country and to deliver his message for the benefit of the common people. After attaining *nirvana*, he seemed to be a totally changed person, both internally and outwardly. Most people who saw him were drawn towards him because a dazzling radiance reflected at his countenance. It is also believed that he did not speak much for a good number of days after he attained *nirvana*. It is quite amazing that after a few days when he left Gaya, all of a sudden, his five companions met him. They had left him earlier, thinking that he would never be able to reach the end of the road in his quest of finding tranquillity. They were still engaged in stern practices to attain the goal of life in the Deer Park near Benaras, which is now known as Sarnath, a great pilgrimage site for the Buddhists. When the companions caught sight of him from a distance, they decided not to give him much attention. But as he came closer, they were awe-stricken to see an unusual radiance at his face. They had never witnessed such a captivating sight before. As he reached within their reach, they became tempted to meet him. Perceiving an unusual serenity at his face, they were certain now that Siddhartha was not the same person whom they had left with disgust. He certainly looked enlightened. They were now ready to listen to him whatever he had in his mind.

Buddha seemed to be pleased to see his old companions after a great lapse of time. The companions insisted that he must tell them all what he had attained after all that hardship, meditation and deep concentration. When he held a brief initial discourse with them, they seemed to be happy for they felt that they had abruptly found in him an outlet for their own liberation. After a short pause, he explained to them all what he learnt during the process of attaining the Enlightenment. He told them that as he possessed a strong determination and consistent concentration, he was able to enter *nirvana*, the state beyond any dismay or sorrow. Listening to such an unusual discourse which also appeared true and convincing to them, they suddenly became restless to learn all about his experience. They implored him to teach them whatever he discovered through his extraordinary journey that led him to his liberation.

The Vital Precepts

Thus, Buddha started his work of teaching the *dharma* first with his five old companions. It was the Deer Park near Benaras on the banks of the Ganges that he gave his first sermons to follow the path of *dharma* which could lead to end human sorrow. It was here that he first explained the Four Noble Truths which promised to deliver human beings from the unending misery to endless bliss. He started with simple things, which most people knew well. Initially, they did not feel convinced that all what he was preaching, could be the main cause of human misery. It greatly alarmed them for they had never thought that things like their longings and cravings could be the main cause of their endless dilemma. Most people even today do not think that way and go on amassing wealth, status, happiness, by fulfilling their own selfish interests, which in fact are short-lived and become source of misery.

Buddha said that the things that people loved and desired most were the main source of their unhappiness. He held that the entire human world was sick because of their unending desires. He also confirmed that it was their *karma* which kept the wheel of birth and death ever rotating on account of the unceasing desire for ego satisfaction of every kind. He declared that he had come to the world as a redeemer to help people prepare themselves to understand the cause of their misery and to remove it for ever to enter the realm of endless bliss. He discovered that the profound truth was extremely difficult to perceive. It seemed even more difficult to believe that tranquillity could not be achieved only through reasoning. He firmly held that it could only be seen and experienced by a wise mind. Those who longed for pleasure and loved to possess it would hardly know that their longings were caused by their conditioning.

Jiddu Krishnamurti, two thousand five hundred years after Buddha, spoke in a similar vein. He said that if people wanted to attain happiness or peace of mind, they must understand their conditioning. Without knowing one's conditioning, one could never stop refraining from longings. To destroy one's conditioning, one simply needed to sit, meditate and start emptying the mind from thoughts that invaded it constantly. If once the mind could be emptied of the wanton thoughts, one would experience unusual peace and strength, never experienced by the individual before. It was the only way to stop the wheel of birth and rebirth and to acquire happiness. (16: p.23) It is said that Krishnamurti did not read from any ancient thinkers or spiritual leaders, yet he spoke about the truth in the same manner what Buddha had said much earlier to him. Like a physician, Buddha unfolded the cause of misery and disclosed that misery could be removed if people followed simple ways. It led to his discovery of the Four Noble Truths.

The Four Noble Truths

1. The first truth was: That human **suffering is a condition that all experience in this world. All desire to achieve happiness. It is the main condition, which causes human suffering.** Since life is implicit with change, it can never satisfy one's increasing desires. Unhappiness increases on account of ever-increasing desires. In this world, everything is suffering. Birth is suffering, death is suffering, and grief is suffering. It is one's craving that gives birth to fresh rebirth. As one's yearning takes place on account of visual objects, sounds, tastes, and mind objects, craving takes root and leads to give birth, death and rebirth. Thus, amid the chain of craving, the cycle of birth and rebirth takes place bringing unhappiness instead of happiness.

2. The second truth was: That every kind of **suffering comes on account of ongoing human possessiveness.** It is **on account of our demands on life that cause suffering.** It is on account of our thirst to acquire more what we dearly love to possess, that suffering is caused. One must clearly know that the cause of grief is one's selfish desires. It is one's thrust to acquire what one wants to possess, that brings suffering. Most people reckon, that life can make them happy if they can acquire what they desire and it would bring them happiness. But people often forget that running after fulfilling their own satisfaction, would always lead them to unhappiness and bring them suffering.

3. The third truth was: That if **one can understand one's greed and longing for possessiveness, one can overcome such feelings.** If one can **understand the cause of suffering,** it can help in ending the suffering. The physician first tries to understand the cause of the disease, then he tries to treat it. Any ailment or disease that can be understood, can also be cured. Sometimes people react without properly understanding the cause of their reactions. Once they know the cause, they may not react in the way they normally do. It would surely help them maintain better relationships. Likewise, if the cause of the suffering is well understood, it could be treated or lessened to a large extent. Just in the manner one can stop reacting oddly by understanding the cause of one's rage, so also one can shun one's longings and selfish desires. When the mind is free from selfish desires, it enters the state of wakefulness. It is also the state of liberation. The extinction of hate, the destruction of greed and delusion, is simply called *nirvana*. One, who has understood all the disparity existing on this earth, he is no more disturbed by anything in the world. He alone is peaceful, completely free from sorrow, anger, and longing and can reach beyond birth and death. It is the state of *nirvana*.

4. The fourth truth was: That **one's selfishness, desire to acquire, longings leading to attachment can be removed by following the Eightfold Path.** This path can lead to change human conduct, change one's viewpoint, and provide a new outlook and a new pattern of behaviour. The stages of the Eightfold Path gradually correct one's state of delusion and help removing the cravings that do not permit the individual to conceive the real nature of 'the self' and 'the universe'. It simply helps one to seek unity with the 'self'. These stages are discussed here.

(i) Right understanding
(ii) Right purpose
(iii) Right speech
(iv) Right conduct
(v) Right livelihood
(vi) Right effort
(vii) Right mindfulness
(viii) Right meditation or concentration

It was an unusual way for redemption and to end the human suffering. So far the prevailing viewpoint to achieve *moksha* or liberation had been quite different. The popular belief was that one could attain liberation by reaching the realm of the supernatural through devotion and prayer. If one could have His *darshan* (vision), the desired liberation could be attained. Buddha's path was entirely different from that in the sense that it did not involve any supernatural power to intervene and help humans to get redeemed. What Buddha had suggested was entirely in human hands. His discovery of the fact that there was misery in the world, and if it was understood properly, it could be removed, was a remarkable finding. He also advised that there was a way to proceed to remove it. These were Buddha's basic precepts. He took forty-five years of his life to teach them and to spread *dharma* in the world to help humans to be free from their misery. The only path he suggested was to follow the Eightfold Path so that one could keep in line with the *dharma* suggested by him.

The Eightfold Path

Buddha first started with *right understanding.* He held that if change was a fact of life, one must not stick to one's longings.

By 'right understanding' he meant to see life as it was. With this right thought, one must understand that happiness could not come from outside. It would come from inside by knowing it clearly that all things were transient in this world. Only this kind of right understanding would help developing wisdom that could enlighten one and help remembering that one must not crave for happiness.

As soon as one possessed right understanding, *right purpose* would ensue from it. Only a wise person knows the purpose of life. Most humans wander in quandary without knowing what aims in life will provide them success and happiness. It is because of that inadequate understanding on their part that they go on pursuing materialistic gains. When one aim (desire) is fulfilled in respect of materialistic gain, one does not stop there. Craving to get more and more goes on accelerating. Thus, Buddha considers that man must have some purpose of life. The purpose of life cannot be anything else than to attain liberation from the cravings that lead to acquire more. Consequently, it results in sorrow. Therefore right purpose means willing, desiring and conceiving only that which keeps one on to the right track.

Right purpose also helps to lead one to *right action*, *right occupation* and *right speech*. In fact, if one's purpose in life is correct, it will surely lead one to choose right profession. He will act rightly and help in cultivation of right speech. One, who has right purpose in life, will have agreement with one's life. Such an individual will not only speak kindly, but will also act compassionately. His mission in life would be not to live to satisfy his own selfish ends but to help others. Buddha holds that all living beings love life and all creatures desire to shun pain. So we must avoid harming others for none like to bear pain and sorrow. Buddha refutes to earn one's livelihood at the other's expense or even support those who harm their fellow beings. *Dharma* (duty) of a human being is not to harm anyone but to protect and help everyone.

Thus, Buddha holds that it is the mind that plays a great role to keep humans in line with the prescribed course of *dharma* (right path). 'We are what we think,' are the famous lines of his first verses in the *Dhammapada*. Our life is totally shaped by our mind. It is such an extraordinary thought that it tells the whole story of one's future life. If one strongly decides to choose a particular profession in life, and follows right means to get it, one can hardly fail in acquiring happiness in one's life. It can happen only if one possesses right thoughts. Suffering will follow only if one cultivates evil thoughts.

Therefore, if one keeps on putting *right efforts*, one will never follow a wrong road. Consequently one will never experience sorrow. Those who really desire happiness in life must train their minds to cultivate right efforts so that in thought, word and action they remain upright. One who desires to attain liberation, it is imperative to try very hard to reach that goal. One cannot reach that goal without putting in right efforts ceaselessly.

Thus, walking correctly through the Eightfold Path prescribed by Buddha is the right procedure to reach the highest goal in life. By following that path, one can gradually attain the internal bliss. Buddha prescribed the Eightfold Path after a lot of thinking. Each step looks connected to the other. Right understanding will provide right purpose, which in turn will help cultivating right thinking, right speech and right ideas to choose right profession. All this will lead to put right efforts that will lead one to keep *right attention*. It also means *right mindfulness*. Buddha spoke of the power of mindfulness in a very expressive manner. He said, "Mindfulness, I declare, is helpful. All things can be mastered by mindfulness."(14: p. 90) Wise people train their minds to follow one thing at a time. In fact, most people go on wasting the strength of their minds by trying to give attention to so many things at a time. Quite often unwise people leave the matters half-done in thought and action. It results in wasting their precious efforts and time, and ultimately wasting their lives for nothing.

Buddha says that those who follow him must always be mindful and cultivate right thoughts which should be focused on the *dharma.* The mind should always cultivate positive thoughts — the thoughts that help others and are implicit with kindness and compassion. Buddha rightly explains how to cultivate right mindfulness in the *Dhammapada*. He says: 'They are not wise, whose thoughts are not steady and minds not serene, and who do not know *dharma*, the law of life.' But only 'those are wise whose thoughts are firm and minds are at peace and who are not affected by good or bad.'* It is true that it is hard to train one's mind. When the mind is untamed, it wanders in any direction it wants to go. Such minds are unruly as they are not controlled by the self. An individual, who cannot control his mind, is bound to suffer in life. But if one's mind is well-trained and controlled, it will bring both, peace and happiness. Those who possess right mindfulness and whose minds are well-trained can lead to meditation or *right concentration*. Buddha says that only they, whose minds are well-trained and who are mindful to *dharma*, are awake. 'They are awake and free from fear.' He further adds to it, 'A well-disciplined mind does greater good.'**

**The Dhammapada*: The chapter related 'On Thoughts'

***The Dhammapada*: The chapter related 'On Thoughts'

Thus, it is imperative to train one's mind and cultivate right thoughts. It would help the individual to meditate with full concentration. When the mind is well-trained through right concentration (meditation), and has emptied itself from any thoughts, selfish passions would not enter into it. Only such a trained mind can cultivate calmness and enjoy serenity.

The Middle Path

Before concluding this chapter on the Basic Precepts of Buddha I would like to include one more important precept from Buddha's teachings. Without including it at this place, this chapter would not be complete. It is the principle he learnt at the time when he had gone extremely weak on account of keeping fasts for several days. When Sujata offered him some rice pudding, he had gone extremely weak and was unable to perform even his routine duties. After eating that pudding, when he gathered some strength, a thought seemed to have flashed through his mind. 'Without a healthy body, one's mind would also become weak and would not work as desired.' Therefore, he decided to relinquish extreme austerity which simply punished the body and decided to keep the middle path in all walks of life. To highlight that point I recollect at this juncture one of the parables reflecting Buddha's views on cultivating 'the middle path'.

His disciples belonged to every class of people and came from far and wide. Besides Ananda and his cousin Devdutta who were extremely rich and who had joined the *sangha* after relinquishing everything, Sona, another wealthy person, also joined him. One day Sona decided to go to the forest alone to practise meditation without caring for the wild animals. After some time when Sona had left, Buddha also decided to follow him. Buddha, besides a begging bowl, carried a *vina* (a musical instrument) with him. In a short time, he found out the place where Sona was meditating. Buddha had totally loosened the strings of *vina* before meeting Sona. When he saw Sona, he asked him to play on the *vina*. Sona took the musical instrument with reverence and tried to play on it. Then amid a mild laughter, he said to Buddha that he was unable to play on it as its strings were too loose. Listening to it Buddha tightened the strings too hard and asked him to play on it. Sona could not play on it once again as the strings were too tight. He told the Blessed One that the instrument required right kind of tuning to make music. Receiving Sona's reply Buddha smiled and said to him that the same rule was applied in seeking *nirvana*. 'Don't let yourself be relaxed and don't let you stretch to break down. Always adopt the middle course, which is the right way to proceed on to the Eightfold Path.'

These were the basic concepts of the right way of life, which Buddha carried on to preach the people for forty-five years. When once he decided to spread *dharma* among his people, he started wandering and preaching extensively. It was on account of his noticeable radiance lurking on his face and his fresh vigorous teachings, that a great number of devotees and followers were attracted to him. As he announced that he possessed the truth that could bring peace and bliss to all, the number of his followers increased conspicuously. He then organised these earliest disciples into groups of monks whom he sent forth on their travels to distant lands to spread his message of *dharma*. He commended the disciples to go forth into the world, and explain the nature of the truth for the profit of many and for the happiness of all. That was all he could do for he possessed love and compassion for the mankind. He also firmly believed that if not all but at least there would be some who would surely understand his teachings, follow them, and attain liberation.

CHAPTER THREE

The Path of Dharma

It is important to note that the followers and the disciples, whom Buddha sent far and wide to spread his message and teachings, were not missionaries like the messengers of other religions who, by different means and ways spread their religion and even forced people to accept their faith if need arose. The followers of Buddha simply declared that their faith consisted of a self-evident truth, which was like a scientific fact and could be experienced and tested if followed earnestly. As people started pursuing his teachings and practising the prescribed procedure religiously, they could see that what Buddha had said was true to a great extent. It soon resulted in multiplying the number of his followers. Thus, for forty-five years, he went on spreading his tidings of peace and love through examples and suitable parables well knitted in a simple and fascinating language. All that attracted several kings and rulers of his time to become his ardent disciples. **In this chapter some of his very important messages, mostly contained in the *Dhammapada*, are unfolded for the benefit of the reader. Although it is not all what he expressed to lead a sane life, yet most of his important precepts and parables that could help to lead a highly contented and peaceful life, are presented here for the benefit of the reader.**

Buddha advised his followers to repeat a simple three-point principle after they had decided to become his disciple. He also asked them to promise and try hard to renounce their attachment towards the materialistic things of the world. The three-point precept that he had suggested to recite regularly, is still recited by the followers of Buddha throughout the world.

1. *Buddham saranam gachami:* I take my refuge in Buddha
2. *Dharmam saranam gachami:* I take my refuge in the *Dharma* (Teachings)
3. *Sangham saranam gachami:* I take my refuge in the *Sangha* (Monks' Community)

Such practices not only founded an order of dedicated and most faithful followers of Buddha, but also predicted a solid support to him as it was a proof that his ideas about *dharma* and liberation were well taken by the people. Quite often he preached the ideas contained in the *Dhammapada*, which is an outcome of his inner voice. Many of the parables, presented in this part of the book, are well connected with the occasions when he was extensively busy in helping people to understand his philosophy. The tales narrated by his disciples who heard them from his mouth, are highly inspirational and educative. If taken seriously, they can easily help changing a person who is really desirous to get transformed and choose to follow the way Buddha had suggested.

Cultivate Positive Thinking

This is the introductory canto of the *Dhammapada* in which Buddha presents his ethical views through simple twin verses indicating how good and bad deeds of an individual bring happiness and sorrow as a consequence to his actions. The *Dhammapada* is surely meant to transform human lives if one understands it well and acts in line with Buddha's wise reflections.

This part of the verses present pairs of thoughts each leading to varied kinds of results. First he indicates the negative kind of likelihood relating to human longings and base conduct. Then he presents the positive sort of possibility, which is hard to follow but surely brings positive results.

> *We become what we think. Suffering follows an evil*
> *thought as the wheel of a cart follows the oxen that draw it.*
> *We become what we think. Joy follows a pure thought*
> *like a shadow that never leaves.*

Perhaps the first lines of the first verse contained in the *Dhammapada* convey the essence of Buddha's teachings. How true it is that 'man becomes only what he thinks'. In this manner, he advocates how one wrong thought can lead to an erroneous action resulting in unhappiness and dolefulness, and how right thought and action provide happiness helping to conquer the base feelings. It is the base thoughts and feelings that distort our lives. In the second verse, he advises to relinquish hatred not by remembering ugly thoughts like 'how someone robbed me or how he attacked me, but by cultivating right thoughts'. All kinds of negative thinking result in hatred only. If one does not cultivate negative thoughts, it is certain that one will be free from hatred. Hatred can never be put to an end by hatred. Instead, it is love that can put an end to it.

There is another analogy in the next verse with the example of a mendicant who bears saffron robe without purifying his mind, and lacks truthfulness and self-control. Such a mendicant is not fit to wear the saffron robe, unless he is endowed with truth and keeps self-control. It is the wise who knows what is essential and crucial for him. Only such a person can set his thoughts on the supreme goal and attain the highest knowledge.

Buddha advocates through simple verses that only selfish people suffer in this life and in the next. They suffer when they see the results of their evil actions. Consequently they receive more suffering in the next life too. Only those, who are unselfish, rejoice in this world and after it. They rejoice from the results of their own actions. Joy awaits them in this life and the next as well. Buddha also rejects simply reciting from the scriptures without practising the advice contained in them. To him, it is only counting cowherds. Those who even know few scriptures but practise the teachings contained in them, and overcome lust, hatred and delusion, only they live in peace and enjoy the spiritual life. Socrates, Martin Luther and Jiddu Krishnamurti also advocated the same ideology and insisted on practising the good rather than simply repeating it orally or reciting it from the books.

Buddha holds that 'a less vigilant person may indulge in sloth and lustful activities. One who is watchful and meditates earnestly, he attains the highest happiness. It is the earnest spiritual aspirant and seeker of the final goal, and who dislikes laziness, he advances like fire and burns all his fetters created by ***karma***. Such a person will never lose the track and will reach ***nirvana***'.

On Being Wise

In the *Dhammapada*, on the subject related to 'Wise Man', Buddha clearly identifies the wise from the unwise person. The Revered One says: As a great rock is not shaken by the wind, the wise man is not shaken by praise or by blame. He adds further: Good people keep on walking towards the goal whatever happens. They refrain from speaking vainly and stay collected in good and bad fortune. Thus, the Enlightened One was never affected by adversaries or was never elated when gains or praises were showered upon him. At times when angry people approached him to pull him down Buddha never expressed any anger towards them. On the contrary, he kept totally calm and displayed an extraordinary serene disposition. When two agitated Brahmins once approached him and hurled filthy abuses, not only he calmed them down by his amazingly un-reactive demeanour, but also accepted them as his disciples later on when they requested him to be his followers. That parable shall be narrated in this chapter later on at a more appropriate opportunity.

While reflecting on the theme related to 'Mind', Buddha highlights the importance of controlling one's mind in the *Dhammapada*. He states most candidly that 'stabilising of one's mind requires cultivation of extreme watchfulness. If one cannot do so, the mind gets fragmented. Mind is mostly restless, unsteady and difficult to guard or control. It is the wise man, who keeps a watch over the mind. It is extremely hard to perceive it. It is so artful and difficult to control as it alights where it desires to alight. Only one who is watchful can protect the mind and get happiness through it. To this thought-process a beautiful parable is related to the life of Buddha when he encounters the most wretched and gruesome person called Angulimal. Angulimal had committed several murders and he was fond of wearing garlands made from human fingers. When Angulimal heard about Buddha's spiritual attainments, he became extremely restless, probably also because he possessed apathy towards the wise and the good, for he was totally a wretched person. Consequently, he could not resist the desire to meet him with the ill intentions to kill him.

After learning about the place where Buddha mostly stayed during the time of the year, Angulimal reached there. As soon as he perceived Buddha, he ran to catch him. But he was surprised to observe that Buddha was also running in front of him as if he were trying to escape him. When Angulimal saw him running away, he tried hard to run faster so as to grab him. The faster he ran to get the Enlightened One it seemed to him that he (Buddha) was running equally fast. After a long chase, when Angulimal was totally exhausted and was unable to follow him any more, he shouted loudly, "Stop running away, coward. The moment I catch you, I'll kill you." Listening to Angulimal's remarks the Revered One said to him very politely:

"Angulimal, it is you who is running. I am just stationary."

Buddha was right. It was only Angulimal who was running, not Buddha. Perhaps because Buddha possessed a kind and compassionate nature, he decided to liberate Angulimal from his gruesome state of mind. So he let him come closer. As soon as he came close, Buddha touched him at his forehead. It is said, that very moment Angulimal felt that he was a changed man. He experienced that all of a sudden he woke up from a deep sleep. After that incidence, Angulimal changed completely. Not only he abandoned killing people, but he also became Buddha's ardent devotee and attained the state of liberation gradually by practising the prescribed *dharma*.

Buddha holds that one who is a wise person should be truthful, and possess no arrogance, deceit, or hate. One who is wise must also not be a miser, and should be away from the evil of self-indulgence. To keep one's mind cool, it is imperative that one controls sleepiness and lethargy. Such a person must not involve in lying and be away from attachment towards forms. A wise person always keeps his pride away and does not involve in violence. He is not excited by what is old or new. Such a person does not grieve when visited by losses and is not controlled by desires. (Adapted from *Sutta-nipata*)

At one such occasion, when the monks were eagerly waiting to hear something inspirational from Buddha, he addressed them by relating a parable he named as 'The Parable of The Raft.' He said to the monks that he was narrating 'The Parable of the Raft' to them to not merely helping them getting across the delusion of the world, but to refrain from certain things that were negative in thought and action and needed their restraint. He unfolded that suppose there was a man who wanted to go across the great stretch of water that came on his way while going on a long journey. The stretch of water was full of dangers and fears on this side, but the other side of the stretch looked safe and without any danger. There was neither a boat to cross nor any bridge to go over the stretch. He decided to make a raft out of sticks and branches of the trees. With that raft, he crossed over to the other side which was fairly safe and secured.

When he crossed the stretch with the raft a thought came to his mind why should he not carry the raft with him on his head as it was of great use to him. At this point Buddha ended his story and put a question to the monks, "What do you think, monks? That the man is doing what should be done to the raft."

The monks after listening to his question replied, "No, lord."

Buddha was pleased to hear it and commented that the man must not carry the raft with him and should leave it there. Then he said that with that parable he had taught them *dharma* and to cultivate right thinking. Good things were great like the raft for getting across but not for retaining. By understanding the parable of the raft the monks should not cling to the right states of the mind and, at the same time, must also not cling to the wrong states of mind. (Adapted from the *Mahima Nikaya*)

Similarly, each set of verses contained in the *Dhammapada* unfolds Buddha's genius, brilliance of mind and pragmatic thinking that approaches life from entirely a different perspective. So far none before Buddha had conceived the idea that it was one's mind that was capable of providing happiness or misery. With this, he also discovered that human misery could end if the mind was used in a positive way. The entire verses in the *Dhammapada* are implicit with such themes which simply tell us about 'how to think righteously and ethically, how to avoid unhappiness which mostly comes as a result of misconceptions, misunderstandings, misdemeanour and immaturity of the mind.' Buddha holds that 'one does not need any hell or afterlife to find the devil. One requires a wise mind to repel the devil. It is the mind itself, which is the realm of the devil. On account of strong longings, the mind is hardly in control. It moves about as it likes. To obey the right will or consciousness, one requires a great training. But this kind of training is very difficult. It requires a lot of patience, hope and determination, as emptying the mind from the ill-conceived thoughts is a very difficult task.'

Promote Maturity of Mind

Buddha holds that unless the mind is controlled through strict training, it cannot possess maturity. An immature mind cannot help to travel on to the right path. Jiddu Krishnamurti, perhaps, has a different view in this respect. He holds that the mind does not require any training to travel in a particular direction. If one has the determination, one can empty the mind from the oncoming waves of thoughts. What one needs is to stop permitting consciously the entry of any kinds of thoughts. When it is done successfully, it is an empty mind which he calls a 'silent mind'. It is also the state of meditation according to Krishnamurti. (16: p. 23) It may, perhaps, be easier for a highly talented mind to empty itself from the constantly oncoming thoughts, but it is beyond the power of an ordinary human being to control the mind abruptly as he has no real idea or training how to refrain from the chain of thought-process that goes on invading the untrained mind. An untrained mind certainly requires training to control it.

Buddha holds that meditation itself is the method of training the mind. Meditation gradually allows access to a level of awareness, where the firm shapes created by thoughts, are gradually weakened. When such rigid shapes made by the habitual thought-process (conditioning) are stopped, the mind becomes silent. It now has no habit to create images. It is perfectly calm, clear and enormously responsive. It then leads to a free action which is backed by free thinking. Thus, Buddha repeatedly embarks upon the idea of cultivating right thinking. He says, "Those who can direct (control) their thoughts are free from the clutches of devil." Every canto in the *Dhammapada* depicts his ideas that insist upon cultivating right habits of thinking. In the theme which tells about how to develop a 'Matured Mind' Buddha, while indicating how to attain *nirvana*, clearly remarks: Desire the path that leads to *nirvana*. Avoid the road that leads to profit and pleasure. One must remember that one always needs to strive hard to cultivate wisdom. He holds strongly: Only a wise and a matured mind can lead to liberation by following the right path.

Follow the Path

In the chapter on the theme related to 'The Path', in the *Dhammapada*, special emphasis has been placed on the idea that it is Buddha who has shown the path but its application and following depends on the individual. Buddha conceives that the Eightfold Path is only the best path and the four known truths are really the best truths. This path discovered by Buddha is certainly helpful to purify one's vision. He reflects verily that there is no other path that leads to cleansing the mind. Only this path leads to end the suffering. Thus, at each step, Buddha installs that his way is the only way that can lead to endless happiness. In order to stay straight on to the path he recommends restraining one's thoughts, words and deeds. For these three — thoughts, words and actions, can discipline one's mind and direct it towards the right path.

Once again, Buddha in the chapter on 'The Self' in the *Dhammapada*, remarks candidly that one who is a responsible person he is conscious and fully aware of the consequences of his actions. He is not only intelligent and wise by being aware of the results of his actions, he is also self-controlled. He adds to it that if one desires to teach others, it is imperative that one should have self-control. He amplifies further: It is so easy to cultivate bad thinking and consequently easier to indulge in bad actions. But it is so difficult to practice positive thinking and to act in a manner that would be beneficial and good to others. He comments: Learn what is right. Teach others only after that. If one does so, one is wise.

Most of Buddha's discourses contained in Pali Canon are mainly directed at the monks who had accepted the Order. But the verses in the *Dhammapada* are primarily meant for the good of the common person. The thought-process contained in those verses is so lucid, that it can be understood easily by anyone who is attentive and desirous to help oneself. Primarily all the material is directed to train the mind and to become good. For once if the mind is trained, it attains wisdom. And when the mind has wisdom, it only acts wisely and rightly. Thus by acting rightly and following the right path, one can always reach the realm of *nirvana*.

Buddha created the *Dhammapada* for the benefit of the common persons because he was committed to help them. He had an unending compassion and love for the suffering humanity. He had also defeated Mara right at the point when Mara had questioned him of the advantages of his findings. Buddha was confident that if not all people then surely most of them would listen to him and would be redeemed. Perhaps that kind of thought gave birth to the *Dhammapada*. The verses seem to be created by an extraordinarily intelligent mind, none other than Buddha's, that can clearly see that it is the human mind which plays the good and bad roles and can provide happiness and misery to the people. Perhaps Buddha created the *Dhammapada* in the same manner as Sri Krishna created the *Bhagwat Gita*. Both had the same mission in their minds — 'emancipation of the common man'. Hence, it is important to read the *Dhammapada* with an open and determined mind so that the desired goals in life could be achieved. What else would be a better way to lead one's life than to follow the path of *dharma* prescribed by Buddha? If one's life is not meant for the benefit of others, it has really not much meaning.

Refrain from Anger

While commenting on the theme of anger in the *Dhammapada*, Buddha unfolds:

Abandon anger, leave pride; trounce all attachment. No unhappiness occurs to him who does not adhere to name and form. Buddha strongly advised to control anger through gentleness and by abandoning unkindness through kindness. He strongly held that evil could be won by good only.

At one occasion, while unfolding how anger could be demeaning, Buddha easily treated an arrogant person who was insolent and highly selfish too. A befitting parable related to Buddha's thought-process advocating how to control one's anger is given here below for the kind reference of the reader. It provides us an idea that Buddha possessed an extraordinarily wise and a calm demeanour. It also depicts how he reacted when encountered by difficult circumstances.

An incident took place when Buddha's spiritual activities were at their pinnacle. Being in possession of an intelligent mind, he reacted most wisely when faced with the problems created by his enemies, mostly Brahmins, who were primarily jealous of him on account of his growing fame and increasing number of followers.

A faithful wife of a Brahmin would often chant '*Buddham saranam gachami*'. That simply meant that she held Buddha in great esteem and revered him as someone supreme, in whose refuge she would always like to stay. She was regularly chanting the precept for many months but her Brahmin husband did not pay any heed to it. One day, on account of a certain odd incident, when the husband's temper was unusually disturbed, he came home earlier with a distressed mind. As soon as he entered his house, the wife opened the door and chanted, as usual, *Buddham saranam gachami*. Listening to it, the agitated Brahmin started hurling abuses towards his wife. He said rather in an agitated mood:

"You wretched woman, how dare you utter the name of my enemy so frequently in my house with reverence, even though you know that he is my rival!" The woman did not react to her husband's chiding, but once again uttered the same precept with an utter calmness. It infuriated the man further. In great anger and aggressive attitude he retorted to her, "I am going to test how great is your Buddha whom you keep on remembering every moment." Saying it, he left his house hurriedly and rushed to see Buddha to test him.

When the Brahmin reached Buddha's hermitage, he started talking to him wildly. Buddha did not react to his filthy language. On the contrary he kept on his usual serenity. When the Brahmin calmed down as if the store of his abusive speech had exhausted, Buddha smiled and bade him to sit. But the Brahmin refused to sit until Buddha would not reply his questions. Buddha looked at him with an enquiring eye and asked him politely, "Tell me your question, Brahmin. I shall try to answer it."

After a pause for a moment, the Brahmin asked him, "Can you tell me, what only thing in the world a person needs to abandon in life?"

Looking at the Brahmin with his usual smile Buddha replied briefly, "Anger." Then after a while he continued: One should forsake anger and pride. If one can do so, sorrow cannot touch that man. Such a person, who does not own anything, is never in the bondage of any thing.

Listening to Buddha's reply, the agitated Brahmin immediately calmed down. After a pause for a few more moments, he fell on his knees. Then prostrating in full before him, he implored Buddha to accept him as his disciple. Buddha smiled and welcomed the Brahmin to be his disciple. When the wife learnt that her husband had relinquished home and had become Buddha's disciple, she was extremely happy. She happily continued devoting rest of her life in company with Buddha's thoughts and principles.

It is said that this Brahmin also had a junior brother who was as frustrated and ill-tempered as his senior brother. When he heard that his elder brother had taken refuge in Buddha and entered his Order, he was out of rage. He darted to see Buddha at once. On reaching the hermitage, he started shouting loudly, hurling filthy abuses which could badly hurt anyone. When Buddha heard someone shouting in an abusive language, he came out of his abode to face the man hurling filthy language. Buddha had not really seen him before. The moment the agitated Brahmin looked at Buddha, he easily recognised him for his countenance bore an extraordinary radiance. The enraged man was now out of his wits, but he continued vomiting abuses with a greater speed that contained more filthy diction. Buddha stood calmly in front of the angry man until the entire store of his abuses exhausted.

When the man became silent, the Revered One asked him, "Brahmin, do you receive guests sometimes in your house?"

"Yes, we do," replied the Brahmin.

"Then, you do prepare delicious food for them," uttered Buddha.

"Yes, we do," replied the man.

"If the guests refuse to eat that food, do you throw it away or keep it with you?", inquired Buddha.

"We keep it with us," replied of the Brahmin.

"So all the abuses you have hurled so far are not accepted by me. Better keep them with you," said Buddha smilingly.

Listening to Buddha's unusual answer, the agitated man calmed down at once. He felt ashamed and like his elder brother he too fell on his knees. Asking Buddha's pardon, he expressed a sincere desire to become his disciple. It is said that later on he was known as one of the most devoted followers of Buddha. Thus, it was entirely the game of the mind to stay calm when faced with strange circumstances. Only the wise and the enlightened like Buddha can keep composed during such odd situations created by both the agitated Brahmins. Sri Krishna, in the Second Chapter of the *Bhagwat Gita*, also expresses similar views on shunning down one's anger for it ultimately destroys the finer qualities of one's mind, making it incapable to identify the right from the wrong when encountered with wanton thoughts.

The Five Precepts

During several occasions, Buddha liked to revise some of his precepts for the benefit of his monks so that they keep on adhering to the principles of *dharma* and attained the desired liberation. Such discourses were commonly held during the rainy sessions when Buddha would retire to the forests and stay there for three months with the band of the monks until the rains ended. Once at such an occasion he told his monks to keep their minds trained and hold five important precepts very dearly if they wanted to follow the path of *dharma*. He said:

1. For the purpose of training one should take a vow to refrain from taking life.
2. For the purpose of training one should take a vow to refrain from taking what is not given to him.
3. For the purpose of training one should take a vow to refrain from sexual misconduct.
4. For the sake of training one should take a vow to refrain from false speech.
5. For the purpose of training one should take a vow to abstain from intoxicants that lead to heedlessness.

These precepts, if followed religiously, are bound to provide happiness, good fortune, liberation, and help cultivating a virtuous life. (Adapted from *Gil Fronsdal*)

Divine Abiding

Once when someone asked Buddha what was meant by 'being divine', he explained it in simple words. He said:

1. When we express love and kindness, this is divine.
2. When we express compassion, this is divine.
3. When we express appreciative joy, this is divine.
4. When we express equanimity in the face of pleasure and pain, this is divine.

He added further that 'a divine way of life was simply found in one's heart, not in submitting to beliefs. It required tremendous devotion to keeping our hearts and minds well adjusted to the circumstances of daily life.' (18: p. 194)

Discover Solutions

Buddha always tried to solve personal problems of his fellow beings by providing them real situations so that they would understand the nature of the problem and solve it themselves. A great parable, first heard by the monks from the Blessed One and later on passed on orally to the people, is reported here under.

Gotami's parents were poor. So after her marriage when she joined her husband's family, she was treated with less respect. After some time, she gave birth to a son. Then they started giving her some respect. When the boy was a few years old and started playing in his courtyard, one day he fell ill and died. It filled the entire family with sorrow. Gotami's sorrow knew no bounds. Not only she lost her only son whom she loved so dearly, she also feared that she would not be treated well at the in-laws place any longer. She, therefore, collected her deceased son, took him in her lap and started moving door to door begging to receive help. She requested every door to give her some medicine to treat her son. People knew it well that there was no medicine for the dead. So they did not give much heed to her request. When they told her that the son was already dead and there was no cure for him, she would not understand them as she was so overwhelmed with sorrow. While she was struggling hard to get some medicine for her dead son, she encountered a wise man who quickly comprehended her situation. He thought that the woman was badly driven out of her mind on account of dolefulness. He affectionately advised her to see a wise person, a sage, who resided at a neighbouring monastery. "Just go to him and ask for the medicine."

Believing the wise man, Gotami carried her son on her hip, and gradually reached Buddha's hermitage. When she looked at the Blessed One, she felt assured that he would surely treat her son. She told him from a distance that she needed some medicine for her son. The Blessed One knew what was wrong with her son. He told her, "Gotami, you did well in coming here for medicine. Now go round the city and bring a handful of tiny seeds of mustard from any house where no one has ever died."

The woman was overwhelmed with the idea that someone might give her the mustard seeds and her son would surely recover from his deep sleep. She told Buddha that she would do that and departed to seek the seeds. She then approached each door situated far and wide and requested the house-owners to give her some mustard seeds so that her son could be recovered. But every householder had the same story. Death had visited every house several times. When Gotami was sure that there was no house where death had not occurred before, she started recovering gradually from her grief. As her emotional stability restored, she went outside the city carrying her dead son on her lap to the burning place. Putting him on the burning pyre, she uttered inadvertently that she now knew the law of the nature. All things that had taken birth must come to an end. All things were impermanent in the world. It was a wise reflection which dawned upon her when she realised the law of the nature. As she learnt it, she understood her acute problem. To remind this fact about life that it was transitory and one who was born must die someday, Buddha always repeated it to the monks. He usually reflected: All formations are transient; all formations are subject to suffering; all things are without a self. (Adapted from *Anguttara Nikaya* & *Samyutta Nikaya*)

Follow Dharma Precisely

When Buddha understood the meaning of *dharma* during the moments he attained *nirvana* under the Bo tree, he conceived quite a different meaning of it than the popular belief rampant at that time. He chose it and used it to describe the goal of human life. For him it meant living in complete harmony with life's cosmic interdependence. Buddha understood the meaning of *dharma* not simply seeing it face to face but repeating the sane activities over and over until he felt that he had reached the unity with the reality. Therefore, he often liked to express his views on *dharma* before his monks to remind them that it was imperative to comprehend its right meaning.

Speaking on the theme of '*Dharma*' in the *Dhammapada*, he expresses most lucidly in one of the verses: *Dharma* is not supported by merely talking about it. It is upheld by actually living — by living in agreement with it. He adds to it that only he, who holds the balance, chooses the good and refrains from the bad practices, follows *dharma* rightly. A beautiful and most educative parable is connected to it in the form of an invocation to the rain god. It unfolds how both, Buddha and Dhaniya, a householder herdsman, get involved in fulfilling their duties and follow inadvertently the Eightfold Path which is essential to pursue if one likes to follow the path of *dharma*. Buddha and the herdsman Dhaniya, invoke the rain god to bring rains as they feel that they have fulfilled their duties, which are absolutely in line with *dharma*. The parable clearly unfolds the activities connected with *dharma* and indicates how a householder can perform his routine duties in view of *dharma* following voluntarily the Eightfold Path prescribed to uphold it.

Dhaniya pointing towards the sky invokes the rain god to come as he feels that he is living in harmony with his fellow beings near the banks of the river Mahi. His house has a roof. Fire is burning inside it and warming it well. Therefore, if the rain god likes to send rains, he will welcome it.

Similarly Buddha invokes rains to come by expressing that he is devoid of anger and free from stubbornness. He has only one night to stay (life is transitory) near the banks of the river Mahi, and his abode has no roof on it. But he possesses no kind of cravings as they are completely extinguished. Therefore, if rains come, it is fine with him.

Dhaniya has no problems right then. He is happy as his cows are roaming in the meadows that are full with green grass, which the cows can eat. So, if the rains come, he will feel delighted.

Buddha adds a few more words in a similar vein. He is equally pleased as with great efforts he has constructed a good raft to take him to the other side of the bank (state of liberation). He has attained *nirvana* and overcome the violent flow of the cravings and desires. The raft, he had made earlier, is no longer of any use to him now as he has already reached the other side of the bank. He is quite happy and therefore, he invokes the rains to come if it pleases.

Dhaniya expresses his joy of life yet in a different way. He is happy as his wife is obedient, sincere and not reckless. She has been living with him cheerfully for a pretty long time. She bears a strong character and is devoid of wickedness. Therefore, he is happy and invokes the rains to come.

Buddha also expresses his happiness through another analogy. He is happy as he has controlled the mind. He has been able to do so after a long and persistent training. He is devoid of any kind of wickedness. Therefore he is blissful and invokes the rains to come.

Dhaniya confirms that he earns his own livelihood with hard and honest means. His children obey him and they are healthy. There is no report against their demeanour and their conduct is good. So if rains come, he would be happy.

Finally Buddha says that he is no one's servant and with the freedom he has gained, he wanders about everywhere in the world without any restraint or with no one to command him. Therefore, let the rains come. (Adapted from the *Sutta-nipata*)

Buddha referred to his teaching simply as *dharma*, which has no single meaning precisely. Its meaning ranges from the term 'idea', to 'reality', and 'truth' to 'law' and 'righteousness'. It is focused mainly on the practice of meditation and involves explanations that are necessary to understand its meaning correctly. Buddha also desires us to practice *dharma* and carry it out in our day-to-day life as it is implicit with the desired ethical code. Such views of Buddha about the practice and the meaning of *dharma* were handed down orally for more than five centuries. Then they were preserved in the ***vinaya*** and ***pitakas***, doctrinal sermons and monistic disciples respectively.

Conceive 'the Self' Correctly

Most parables and the ideas contained in the *Dhammapada* represent Buddha more than a philosopher. His main concern was to discover the way to human liberation and not merely philosophising about it. A Chinese scholar named Garma C.C. also reflects emphatically that Buddha's primary mission in life was to discover a right path to help humans redeem and not merely philosophising.

His primary concern was to point out the way to liberation — liberation from the deep-rooted attachment to a delusory self which is the source of all passion-desires and their resultant pains and frustrations. Philosophical speculations were persistently rejected and denounced by Buddha as useless, foolish and un-salutary. Actually in Buddha's teachings... what we find is a significant therapeutic device, the instruction on how to get rid of the deep ego-clinging attitude. (2: p.31)

He left his royal abode in the middle of the night to discover 'a practical way' to solve the problem of human sufferings. Though most holy people who came before him knew it well that suffering was there in this world, but none had much idea that it was caused mainly by human cravings and by misconceiving the self as a real entity. During his enlightenment, Buddha observed clearly that human longings caused most sufferings. Most people who visited him came primarily to discuss their problems and desired to know how to get redeemed from them. Buddha, in the state of enlightenment, had clearly understood the cause of most of those problems that constantly troubled human mind. He discovered that the suffering mind only required the destruction of that conceited ego through whose role the humans took the unreal as real and suffered as it led to create cravings and deep attachments.

He constantly insisted to oppose suffering whether it was real or imaginary. That could be possible only through the right understanding of the nature of 'the self' and wise interpretation of all human existence. He believed strongly that only an intelligent kind of mind (possessing right understanding) could bring the destruction of every kind of ego formations. It was something new which so far no one had conceived to redeem humans from suffering. The truth is that none had thought so far that the self was not a real entity. In Buddhist traditions, the idea of a separate self or an ego is taken to be merely a scholarly creation. Buddha thought that it was not correct to consider the ever-changing self as real. He concluded that most people did so (identified the self as 'I') because of their ignorance and because it was convenient for them to define the ever-changing combinations of attributes which he identified as *skandhas*.

What is this *skandha* from Buddha's point of view? *Skandha* consists of forms, feelings, perceptions, ideas, wishes, dreams and consciousness. Since there is a constant interplay and connection among the *skandhas*, it provides the effect of giving a false sense of personal identity and continuity. But in reality there is no 'I' existing on its own separately. What it feels like a 'self' is the ever-changing relationship among psychic and physical forces. Buddha often used a simile to identify the self. He identified it with 'a chariot' to express it lucidly. The term 'chariot' does not indicate a simple single reality. It describes something which is constituted by so many small and big parts placed together to crystallise one whole, named a chariot. As no parts of this aggregate (chariot) can be separated off to be called a chariot, in the same manner no part of a human being can be taken apart and called 'the self' or 'I'. The Western philosophers like Schopenhauer, William James, Russell and David Hume had similar views about the self. They considered the mind or the self as a bundle of different perceptions united together by particular relationship. But apart from that there exists a distinct disparity in the opinions of the Western thinkers and than that of Buddha. (12: p.28)

The Western thinkers kept their personal opinions away from their findings and concluded or discovered the truth as it stood true by itself. Buddha had conceived its meaning after attaining 'awareness' through a strict discipline and training. It was his personal experience during the state of enlightenment that provided him the right kind of understanding of the meaning of 'the self'. He said that one's personal ego that seemed so real was not all important to build up an image of 'the self'; these were bundles of thoughts, desires, memories, fears, drives and anxieties that also built that idea of the 'self'. Thus, a lot of mental events temporarily linked with a physical body, provide the meaning of a separate 'self'. This is how Buddha describes personality (the self), which in his view is composed of five ingredients: form, feelings, perception, impulses, and consciousness. Then without referring to any individual self, he stated that, 'birth is the result of these aggregates. When death takes place those aggregates break apart'. He added: Form is the body with which most of us identify ourselves. Thus, he concluded that it was absurd to consider '*the self*' as a real entity.

Buddha always reminded his disciples that 'the self does not have any material shape, nor the material body possesses any self'. He added that 'feelings, perception, the impulses and even consciousness could be erroneously taken as the self. Each of these aggregates is impermanent and leads to suffering. Each of these is non-self and compounded. These aggregates must not mislead them (monks) so that they take them as the self'. He always repeated before his disciples that let no one should take the material shape of the body as real, so that when it changes, they don't get hurt, lament and suffer on that account. (Adapted from *Samyutta Nikaya*)

In the same way, he also did not consider 'the universe' real. Like a modern physicist who now reckons that there is no 'real' universe (like the illusion that a stick looks bent when put in a glass of water), Buddha found 'the universe' made (created) of mind. What he meant by it was that there was no real universe existing apart from our mind or thinking. But this does not mean that the physical reality is not there. What we see in the world is caused by the structure of our consciousness. Besides, 'his findings that all was transitory in the world', was also an unusual discovery. It revolutionised the existing beliefs about the world. Such a discovery was quite alarming and unusual to anyone who listened to him. But he presented such arguments which seemed to be true and convincing, and consequently seemed to be working. Buddha did never like to throw ideas on the people. He always wanted them to realise the truth through their personal experience. Therefore, he always insisted to conceive things correctly.

Buddha candidly reflects in the *Dhammapada* that 'We are what we think'. If someone claims to be a real sage, he has to be worthy of it by striving hard to attain 'awareness'. After attaining awareness, he must act and live by what he has discovered. In fact, in the *Dhammapada,* he reflects emphatically that one who simply talks about his teachings, and does not act upon them is only like a cattleman who feels happy in counting other's cattle. He also reflects in it that only he is worthy to wear a saffron robe who thinks and acts like a sage. Therefore, his claims about his discovery relating to human misery, and his interpretations about the nature of 'the self', and the existence of the universe' seemed to be true as what he said was based on his real experiences. He implored people that anyone who followed the path could also see the truth about his discovery.

Cleanse the Past Karma

The Buddhist teaching, in respect of his discovery of the fact that there is misery in human life, is often misunderstood. The popular charge against it has been that it reflects only pessimism. But his teachings are certainly not pessimistic. He affirms positively that there is misery in this world and all people suffer on account of it, but he also finds a way to overcome that misery. It is a path that he discovers and tests himself. He leads that path also for more than forty years. He firmly holds that the path to attain *nirvana* could easily be followed provided one possesses determination and right training. The path could be followed if one tries hard to walk on it. Besides determination and hard work, one would also require wiping away the past *karma*. In respect of wiping away the past *karma*, Buddha's findings are different from what was rampant during his time. Some critics hold that it is not completely possible to accept in totality that human suffering, which is primarily caused on account of cravings and the past misdeeds, could be wiped out entirely, though to some extent it could be right.

Providing explanations to confirm that his point of view regarding human suffering is not really pessimistic, Buddha states that all life is subject to change. That means human suffering can also be diverted. His most notable reflections in the *Dhammapada*, 'We are what we think,' provide us an idea that human beings can divert their lives away from misery and get liberated, if they cultivate the habit of thinking rightly. Misery can be refuted and happiness can be achieved through wise thinking and right actions. Buddha insisted that 'our thoughts can be subject to control through specific training and practice'. It can certainly help in diverting our attention from the realm of misery and can provide us a right direction leading to attain permanent happiness. That way his teachings do not lead to pessimism.

He strongly affirms that 'the principle of cause and effect' is an ongoing process and ultimately influences our lives. It is an inescapable pattern of life, which cannot be separated from it. 'What you sow, so shall you reap.' Christ also expressed similar views in relation to straighten human conduct. It ultimately leads to direct our views on the theory of *karma*, which leads to consider that we all are subject to be tied down to our destiny, which does not permit us to change our lives from what is already destined. But this sort of criticism against the Buddhist tradition can easily be refuted by Buddha's strong arguments that 'one can change the ways of life by working hard and by following the path he has suggested to attain liberation'.

To this he further adds that it (the path leading to liberation) cannot be achieved only by individual 'will' or strong drive. It (awakening) is also not acquired only through meditation. It can certainly be attained by improving the individual's mental state in which no sign of 'I' or 'mine' thrives. To attain that state of mind, one has to put efforts to clear one's *karma*. To clear the past account of *karma* (bad actions), one must not react to whatever comes to him in daily situations. One has to be kind, compassionate and courageous to take all what comes in life. Then he adds further that *karma* is not wiped away, but bad actions stored in the past can be negated and balanced by positive entries. When the account of the past *karma* is closed, one comes to a point where there is no grieving or sorrow. Then the past is guiltless and *karma* is cleansed, opening the way to liberation.

Stay Awake

Buddha did not simply say it but he did change his life through a strong determination and by erasing the past *karma* by his good and kind actions. Besides, he also actively cultivated compassion and forgiveness and acquired such human virtues that helped him forming good *karma*. He practised hard to follow that path. As a consequence, he was enlightened and became 'awake'. Once, when he was sitting in a meditative posture, concentrating deeply, someone passed by him and was greatly dazzled by the radiance lurking at his face.

He asked him inadvertently, "Are you a god?'

Buddha opened his eyes and briefly replied, "No."

Not satisfied by his brief reply, the man asked him again, "Are you an angel?"

Buddha said again, "No."

The man was curious to know who that radiant man was, so he put another question, "What are you, then?"

The Blessed One smiled briefly and told him, "I am awake."

In other words, Buddha told the enquiring person that he was more concerned with his intellect. In Sanskrit, the literal meaning of the root word *budh* is 'to wake up'. So his reply was absolutely right. He was totally aware and so awake too. Buddha had conquered all his cravings to become aware of his 'self'. In the *Dhammapada*, while reflecting on the theme relating to 'Wakefulness', the Blessed One says that the followers of Buddha are awake day and night as they remember Buddha, remember the Truth of the Law. They remember the holy brotherhood, remember the mystery of life, and find joy in love for all beings. They also find joy in supreme compassion and attain happiness and bliss when they become master of all desires.

It seems easy to narrate the term 'awareness' and to 'be awakened', but all that cannot be achieved so easily by merely practising or by any amount of will, drive or determination. Being awake is quite a difficult task. It requires one's personal identity totally dissolved. The wall between 'the self' or 'I' and rest of the creation needs to be completely dropped. One has to come out of one's evolutionary legacy, age old instincts, conditioning, drives, and all experiences of the primal past, taking off all individual personality and leaving it behind. It is the way to clear one's *karmas*. Then comes awareness and one becomes awake. Connected to this thought-process is a most fascinating parable which needs to be retold at this juncture.

Once when the Blessed One was unfolding his wise reflections and talking about the matters relating 'how to walk on the right path so as to attain freedom,' his three disciples were sitting in front of him listening to his invaluable discourse. One of them was Ananda, his most beloved disciple and a companion as well. When the Blessed One had spent considerably long time with them, Ananda interrupted him politely and said to him humbly,

> "Revered Master, I have been listening to your most invaluable discourse for quite a long time and I find that it is most important for all of us to know all what you have been narrating if we really desire to get redeemed. But my two other companions often go to slumber in between although your discourse is so captivating."

Buddha blissfully looked at Ananda and told him lovingly:

> "Ananda, the two companions of yours are unable to hear all what I have been telling, for their *karma* in the previous life was not as wholesome. They both were butchers by profession and so on account of their previous *karma* they are unable to keep up with my teachings."

Then after pause for a moment, Buddha continued: "But you, Ananda, had a different kind of past life. In your past life, you belonged to a class which was more concerned with learning of scriptures and study of the holy books. As a result, your personal surroundings were always full of spiritual environment. Therefore, your past *karma* has earned much good for you to stay attentive when good matters are discussed." Ananda was much pleased to listen to the answer given by Buddha. This kind of discourse also unfolds his belief in transmigration and theory of cause and effect that crystallise one's *karma*.

Cultivate Compassion

Some thinkers lay a charge against the Buddhist tradition that it is totally deficient in 'love'. This charge can easily be refuted on the grounds that Buddha himself left his happy family and royal status just to discover the remedy for the human misery. Why at all should someone be concerned with others' problems when he has all the amenities of life? But Buddha, from the beginning of his life, was highly compassionate and sympathetic to all those who were weak and who needed his love and care. Related to it is a real event which is connected with his early life when he was still enjoying his royalty and living in the stately palace with a highly caring family.

One day, while he was mounted on his steed, roaming aimlessly with his royal retinue in the nearby forests, a wounded pigeon fell from the sky right in front of him. The prince Siddhartha at once dismounted from his horse and picked up the wounded bird which had been pierced by an arrow. Siddhartha slowly took the arrow out of its body and with great care and tenderness carried it towards his palace. He had hardly gone a few yards that his cousin, Devdutta, who had shot at it, came mounted on his horse and demanded the bird back from the prince. He said that as he had shot at it, he had the right to take it back. But the prince refused to give it to him. The matter was brought to the court. When Siddhartha was summoned to the court by his father to answer why he did not return the bird to his cousin, he replied very humbly: "Sir, I believe that the person who tends someone and helps to bring it to life, has more right on it than the one who is bent upon destroying it."

The reply of the prince was so convincing that the king who was also his father, had to agree with him and allowed him to keep the bird until it was fully recovered from its wounds. Therefore, from the very beginning Buddha was a compassionate person. Besides his teachings, his demeanour always left an impression of kindness and love that constantly influenced people. The truth about it can be found from the fact that most people, belonging to Buddhist lands like Burma, Thailand including Tibet, and all those who are temporarily residing in the northern part of India after their exile from Tibet, are generous, kind and happy sort of people. Things have changed to some extent only since when foreign influence has disturbed their environment.

It is reported that Buddha himself personally undertook a great care of a sick and an unattended monk. He gave him bath and tended him as if he were his own child. He was always terribly disturbed by a personal problem and an unbearable loss that troubled someone. We have already related stories about the wounded bird and of Gotami, who had lost her only son and who became almost crazy on account of her loss. Besides, who would like to relinquish all the royal comforts of life for the sake of discovering solutions for others' problems and misery? Unless one is really a kind and compassionate person, one will never abandon the best comforts of life. Therefore, basically, Buddha possessed a highly compassionate disposition.

There is yet another evidence of his kind and compassionate nature. When Buddha learnt that the food, given by his devotee Cunda, who was a blacksmith, was unwholesome, and which ultimately caused him to leave this earth, he sent Ananda to tell him that Cunda must never blame himself for that food which might cause him die. He said that Cunda was innocent and he would have never given him that food if he knew that it was rotten. It was perhaps a similar kind of expression that the Christ made for the people who crucified him. "Oh God, forgive them for they don't know what they are doing."

Only great people possess an innocent, forgiving, compassionate and loving disposition. Buddha falls in the same category. Or perhaps his category in terms of possessing a compassionate nature is different than that of the others. Was it not totally out of compassion that although he attained *nirvana* long ago, he went on wandering and preaching for the benefit of others, postponing his own final release from the world? Thus, compassion is a virtue which one must cultivate if one desires to attain peace of mind and unending happiness.

Destroy Ego to Attain Nirvana

Buddha holds that the term *nirvana* needs to be differently interpreted than what commonly people take it. It is not merely 'extinction'. What actually extinguishes at the attainment of *nirvana* is only the self-centred and self-assertive life or ego to which ordinary person is inclined to attach oneself considering it as the highest good and the best in life. When all the cravings are lost and totally overcome, the true self is attained. In fact, it is the true self which one starts experiencing or realising in the state of liberation. When *nirvana* is attained, one is able to enter into the intimate fellowship with the whole universe as the limits of the self are now boundless. The horizon of the individual (self) is extended to a limitless reality. There is a total realisation of the self and it becomes one with the universe. It is the only state of enlightenment. Buddha holds that the term 'enlightenment' indicates a direct, vigorous spiritual experience provided through the faculty of intuition. When one's intuition is developed and sharpened by strict spiritual disciplines, serious meditation and contemplation, enlightenment is dawned upon the individual. It is entirely a different state of 'the self' in which it transcends beyond the power and pull of 'the opposites', and fully realises that the universe and the self are one.

How does Buddha describe the process of attainment of *nirvana* to his disciples? During the first watch of the night when he attained *nirvana*, he marked how the person named Siddhartha went back to see his many previous lives. In the second half of the watch, he saw the world as distinctly as if he were looking at it from a clear mirror. He observed innumerable deaths and births of other beings whose life cycles of coming and going into the world depended upon their *karma* crystallised by their past actions. In the final watch, he observed how human cravings caused ignorance by taking untrue as true by looking at one's personality as real, possessed with a physical self. Buddha then tried hard to see how to end the process of suffering. He discovered that its root cause was ignorance, which gave birth to *trishna* (desires), a deep craving for personal satisfaction. Suffering arises because we try to get from life something which is not there. As we go on with those cravings, we suffer consistently. Therefore, unless we refrain from the cravings, our suffering can never end. When our personal sorrow comes to an end by refraining from all desires and attachments, the self transcends to its real state in which all cravings are dissolved. In other words, it is the true state of *nirvana*.

In a state of *nirvana*, a person is no longer subjected by his desires or fears, which crop up from attachments to illusions about life. In that state, a complete inner freedom is experienced, which is a true state of tranquillity. Thus, *nirvana* in Buddha's terms is the search for identifying a person's true self. The conventional belief that the self possesses a body is not true. The self is not permanent and neither it is substantial. Buddha holds that a person is a connection of speedily changing and interacting mental and physical processes. It is difficult to exert total control over those changing processes at a time. Only a partial control can be employed over those processes at a time. So they often change in different ways providing more suffering. It is therefore necessary to go on trying to control them regularly and determinately.

Buddha's active teaching lasted for around forty-five years. During that time he travelled far and wide and with untiring efforts taught the principles that he had discovered to help humans to get redeemed. His ministry attracted all kinds of disciples — kings, farmers, disbelievers (sceptic), householders, courtesans (prostitutes), and highly intellectuals. Considering the social climate of his times, he made a great concession to admit women into his Order at the insistence of his dear disciple Ananda. There is something great in his teaching, which is highly convincing and full of lucidity. When you go through his basic findings seriously, you feel persuaded by his unusual discovery. The 'Truth' that Buddha discovered is perhaps slightly alien than the rampant set of beliefs. It simply requires your personal efforts to achieve it. The state of *nirvana* is not a place in the high heavens, but it lies within you only. It is also not difficult to reach it except that it requires your total faith in the path Buddha had discovered.

I reckon the path is so lucid that if one honestly tries to comprehend the nature of the path and understands the principles implicit in it, it would not be difficult to pursue it. If one can follow it stubbornly, one will certainly reach the realm of the serenity that one has never known before. It is the state

Buddha's bust from a tall statue built in the 12th century in Burma

of *nirvana*. It is the state of liberation as well. It is the only state of enlightenment. The truth is that not only we all carry the seeds of enlightenment within us, but we also possess a natural desire to grow towards it. This urge may be subdued at times within us on account of confusion that is often rampant in our everyday lives. But if we try hard we will certainly respond to it and instinctively know that we are moving in the right direction. It is not just theorising, but it is a matter of direct personal experience too for many people. (19: p.14) Therefore, let us all try hard to attain it.

Buddha says emphatically and repeatedly that whenever there is ignorance in life, suffering has to follow. By subsiding one's ignorance which can happen only when one refrains from cravings and drives, the unreal self comes to an end and the real one transcends. That is the state of *nirvana*. It is the state of enlightenment too.

In the next chapter, I wish to present before the reader in details the various stages of awakening Buddha gradually reached on the night when he attained the total release from the worldly fetters. I shall also try to highlight the attempts of Buddha and Sri Yogananda, another spiritual ascetic in that respect, and will point out the difference in their approaches in the final attainment of a complete liberation.

CHAPTER FOUR

The Stages of Final Attainment

Although Buddha did not explain the actual meaning of enlightenment in clear words, he did narrate very closely and distinctly 'what happened to him on the night when he really attained it'. We have already discussed it briefly under the chapter on "The Path of Dharma". But I would like to give some more details about the experiences he had on that night. Such details are recorded in the *Vinaya Pitaka* (iii.4) from where we learn how he gradually travelled on the road to enlightenment and attained it in four stages during different quarters of that night. I shall also like to present before the reader a comparative view of the nature of final awareness or liberation that Buddha attained and the experiences that Yogananda had during those stages of awareness. Like Sri Yogananda, other spiritual masters like Vivekananda and Jiddu Krishnamurti, also had similar experiences during their final attainments. I simply wish to present it before the reader to highlight how Buddha's and Yogananda's experiences regarding their final awareness were similar and were also slightly different at a certain point.

Experiences before Attaining Nirvana

Legends unfold that during the night he attained *nirvana,* he seated himself to meditate with a firm determination. He decided not to get up from deep concentration until he had reached his goal. Then he focused his complete attention on one point, totally calm, motionless and concentrating his mind away from every kind of selfish urge. After concentrating thus for some time, he entered the first meditative state in which the mind became almost free from divided notions and experienced endless joy. Then the second meditative stage came when he put a complete end to his divided thoughts (no delusion) and concentrated harder one-pointedly. Concentrating thus, when no wave of thought was left in his mind, he experienced the endless joy that projected before his mind the states of unity. As he continued his concentration, he experienced that the joy he had started to experience became more intense and pure. He also became conscious of the depths of his unconscious states of mind. Buddha took it as the third state of meditative experience. Then he reached the fourth meditative state in which he was totally beyond any pleasure and pain. It was the state in which the mind was completely beyond the reach of thought. He reached this state of mind through complete detachment and intense concentration. All these four meditative states of mind took place during the first part of *dhyana* or concentration.

Normally thought follows a path triggered by stimulus and response. Events happen either outside the mind or are triggered in the mind by external stimulus, and create a chain of thoughts in the mind. To break that kind of continuous thought-process created by external or internal stimulus, one needs to concentrate very hard. Buddha had already mastered his mind and crossed easily that stage during the first part of *dhyana* through the four meditative states of mind. Although it looks so simple to reach the first stage of *dhyana* that Buddha attained during the first quarter of that night, it is absolutely difficult for an ordinary person to mount that stage without very hard work and regular practice to concentrate deeply.

In the second stage of *dhyana*, Buddha concentrated further deeper. It helped him to save the mind from all kinds of outside thoughts. It also reduced the distractions to a minimum level. As his concentration increased gradually, disruptions slipped away far into distance. During this state of *dhyana*, Buddha was able to gain detachment from the self-centred conditioning that goes on affecting human beings constantly. 'It is really difficult for an individual to free oneself from the day to day conditioning that leads first to personal fulfilment.' But Buddha could attain that de-conditioning through rigorous meditation and deep concentration. During this stage of *dhyana*, he was able to dissolve all such desires that were created by his selfish interests and which did not let him think to help and serve others.

Buddha, through deep meditation, descended steadily and gradually into the depths of the unconscious. The world of everyday experience seemed to be slipping away from him except that he remained connected to his self with the thin thread of concentration. It was a very difficult state to reach. Only those who work hard and are highly intellectual can reach that stage. When one reaches that stage, the mind gets immense power and each moment of thought comes under its control. It is the moment that comes when the individual is able to understand that all the appearance of continuity in the world is not real but simply confusing like watching a movie and taking all that as real. At this depth of consciousness, the sense and thoughts of personal identity go far away. Then one gets intensely awake to one's inner world — deep in one's unconscious. This was the second stage of Buddha's *dhyana*.

In his third stage of *dhyana*, Buddha reached a state when no thoughts were left in the mind except consciousness, which became like a calm lake, perfectly tranquil, clear and full of joy. It helped him to peep right through the mind into its deeper consciousness. He identified it as *bodhi* which was like a glimpse of pure light followed by immense joy. Buddha discovered at this point that the wall between the self and the rest of the creation was paper-thin. In order to go further, that wall needed to fall. On the other side of the wall lay the collective unconscious. Buddha identified it as a 'storehouse-consciousness' or the 'stockroom of the mind' that stored the seeds of our evolutionary heritage, drives, instincts, urges and experiences of the past. In order to break away from that heritage (conditioned instincts and drives) one required detaching from one's individual personality.

Buddha made it clear that breaking away from the personal identity (I or me), could not be achieved only through concentration and meditation. It required clearing the past accounts through right *karma*. We have already discussed briefly in the Third Chapter how one's bad accounts could be cleared through right activities. To clear our old bad accounts, we have to act with kindness, courage and compassion. Buddha held that the '*karma* is not easily rubbed out, but its negative entries can be wiped out by good entries only'. It takes many lives to clear the account of the bad entries by doing good acts continuously. It is only through good acts that one's past mistakes can be erased. It is a kind of paying back in terms of kind and compassionate acts, which is a normal pattern of spiritual growth that stretches over many lives. Once when all the bad entries are erased, one discovers the unity between the self and the universe.

Then Buddha described the fourth stage of *dhyana*. He clearly stated that the conditioned instincts and drives, though pushed back to a deep remote during the second and the third stages of *dhyana*, did not die completely. Like seeds they could come up again if one did not try hard to stay in the spiritual domain constantly. Like seeds they would appear again if one did not keep in touch steadily with the discovered unity. The experience of unity needs to be repeated again and again until all the seeds are burnt out, holds Buddha. He firmly believed that an individual, desirous to reach *nirvana,* must try hard to reach it constantly. One should always keep the goal to reach the depths of unconscious through constant meditation and good acts. Buddha emphasised that 'even for a second, one should not lose the awareness of the unity. Only then every corner of the mind would be immersed with the blissful light and the thin wall of the conditioned instincts or drives would completely break away. Then a new personality devoid of separateness would emerge. It is the only state of *nirvana*. It is the end of the chain of birth and rebirth. It is the state of unlimited joy,' holds Buddha.

As he reached the fourth stage of *dhyana*, the individual named Siddhartha totally dissolved and the one known as Buddha emerged from it. Buddha had now attained unity with the universe and was completely awake. He recognised this state of consciousness as the state of total awareness. The extent and nature of awareness attained by the spiritual master known world over as Paramahansa Yogananda, is almost the same when he reaches the point of unity with the universe. He calls it 'an experience in cosmic consciousness'. Let us try to learn from Sri Yogananda's account about his personal cosmic experience during which he transcended his physical body and became one with the universe. To highlight the moments of his spiritual experiences, I reproduce one of the incidences that took place in his early life when he was still practising meditation under the guidance of his guru, Sri Yukteswar. (20: p.143-45)

Experience in Cosmic Consciousness

After leaving his guru's abode abruptly for a good number of days when Mukunda* came back to his ashram again, he politely begged his Master's forgiveness for disappointing him by not discharging the *ashram* duties properly. Like any other compassionate and kind teacher, Sri Yukteswar, instantly forgave him. After a few days of his return to the ashram, Mukunda went to his Master's empty sitting room and planned to meditate. He tried hard to concentrate, but he could not control his thoughts as they constantly drifted away from him. His guru was quite aware of the mental state of his disciple. Consequently he called him from a distant balcony. But Mukunda did not respond to him thinking that if he attended to his master's call, he would not be able to meditate. After a while Sri Yukteswar summoned him again. For some time Mukunda did not respond but when the Master called him again firmly, he said to him that he was meditating at that time, so he was unable to come. Listening to the disciple's plea, the Master said loudly, "I know how you are meditating with your mind disturbed like leaves in a storm! Come here to me."

Disappointed and exposed, Mukunda made his way towards his Master. The Master looked at him kindly and spoke, "Poor boy, mountains cannot give you what you want." Then he said to him after a pause, "Your heart's desire shall be fulfilled." (20: p.143) With these words, he gently struck at his chest above his heart. The Master's gentle stroke on his chest brought him the cosmic vision instantly. His body became immovably rooted and breath was drawn out from his lungs. Soul and mind instantly lost their physical bondage and piercing light streamed out like a fluid from his every pore. He felt that the flesh was

* 'Mukunda' was the name given to Yogananda at his birth by his parents.

as though dead, yet in his intense awareness he experienced that never before he had been so fully alive. His sense of identity was no longer narrowly confined to a body but embraced the circumambient atoms. He saw that people on distant streets seemed to be moving gently over his remote periphery. The roots of plants and trees appeared through a dim transparency of soil as he perceived the inward flow of their liquid.

He observed that the entire vicinity lay bare before him. His simple frontal vision was now changed to a vast spherical sight, concurrently perceiving all. Through the back of his head he observed men and animals moving far down Rai Ghat Lane. He also observed that all objects within his panoramic sight trembled and vibrated like quick motion pictures. His own body, the courtyard, the furniture on floor, the trees and sunshine occasionally became violently agitated and finally melted into a luminescent sea. The unifying light alternated with materialisations of form, metamorphoses revealing the law of cause and effect in creation.

It was the moment when his inner self enjoyed an oceanic joy. He experienced: "The spirit of God, I realised, is exhaustless Bliss; His body is countless tissues of light. A swelling glory within me began to envelop towns, continents, the earth, solar and stellar systems, tenuous nebulae, and floating universes. The entire cosmos, gently luminous, like a city seen after at night, glimmered within the infinitude of my being... I saw a mellow radiance, ever undiminished."(20: p.142) Repeatedly Mukunda saw the creative beams condense into constellations, and then gradually resolved into the sheets of transparent flame. He also observed that there occurred rhythmic reversion and sextillion worlds passed into filmy lustre, then fire became firmament. At one point, he noticed that blissful *amrit* (nectar bestowing immortality) flowed though his body in great fluidity.

Then he heard the creative voice of God resounding *Aum*, which he took as the vibration of the Cosmic Motor.

The Basic Difference

If we keep in view what Buddha and Sri Yogananda really experienced during the moments of their awareness, we find that both had almost similar experiences to a large extent. They both felt that their entire body melted and merged into the universe and became one with it. They were able to see everything far and wide in which the scores of creation went on melting into one lucent sea, just like the waves of ocean that after the tempest, dissolve serenely and become one with it forming unity. They both observed that their entire cravings ended at that point of awakening and they enjoyed an endless bliss that they had never experienced before. In that state of enlightenment no thoughts were left out in the mind except consciousness, which became like a calm lake, perfectly tranquil, clear and full of joy. It helped them to peep right through the mind into its deeper consciousness. Buddha discovered during the moments of his awareness that the main cause of suffering was human cravings that triggered the chain of birth and rebirth. It was the law of cause and effect backed by one's *karmic* deeds that finally led to take birth. In order to stop the chain of birth and rebirth one has to erase one's previous *karma* by good deeds, deep and constant meditation and strong determination.

Sri Yogananda discovered similar things during his state of his awakening. He observed that the entire vicinity lay bare before him. His simple frontal vision was now changed to a vast spherical sight, concurrently perceiving all. Through the back of his head, he observed men and animals moving far down Rai Ghat Lane. He also observed that all objects within his panoramic sight trembled and vibrated like quick motion pictures. His own body, the courtyard, the furniture on floor, the trees and sunshine occasionally became violently agitated and finally melted into a luminescent sea. The unifying light alternated with materialisations of form, metamorphoses revealing the law of cause and effect in creation. But Buddha and Sri Yogananda attained enlightenment through different procedures and observed things of different nature too.

1. Buddha attained enlightenment through personal efforts and hard work in one night after passing through four states of *dhyana.* During those different stages of *dhyana* he passed through various states of awareness, transcending step by step from the previous state to the next one. It is said that after becoming perfectly awake, and reaching the pure state of enlightenment, he entered into that state many times that night. Then he discovered that 'one should always keep the goal to reach the depths of unconscious through constant meditation and good acts'. Buddha also emphasised that 'even for a second, one should not lose the awareness of the unity'. Only then every corner of the mind would be immersed with the blissful light and the thin wall of the conditioned instincts or drives would completely break away. Consequently a new personality, devoid of separateness, would emerge. He considered it as the state of *nirvana* and end of the chain of birth and rebirth. All such experiences came to Buddha as a result of his own efforts, devotion, and strong resolution.* To achieve all that he did not receive any external

---

* Except that Buddha learnt practising meditation from a couple of known teachers while wandering in the forests as a recluse to find answers of his questions relating to human suffering, no one taught him the procedure to attain enlightenment.

help from any master like Sri Yogananda, who totally depended on his guru, Sri Yukteswar, to attain self-realisation and awakening.

2. Buddha followed an intellectual path discovered through karma yoga, after wandering in the forests and punishing his body in different ways for seven years. Sri Yogananda from the beginning was in quest of a guru who would help him to walk on that road to reach his goal through *bhakti marg* (devotional way).

   Finally he found his master through whose kind grace he had the first vision of awakening when he was still young.

3. Buddha did not reach his final awakening through any supernatural entity. He simply attained it by his own intelligent thinking. He was an extremely wise person who always exercised reflective thinking to discover answers to his enigmas. It was purely his reason-implicit mind that discovered the path for himself and for the others. It was totally a new way that none had discovered so far. But Sri Yogananda, from the beginning, held that his quest for self-realisation would end only when he reached the realms of God through a guru. In a way it was a predestined way that many had already walked though it before him. Consequently, during his first awakening in his guru's *ashram,* he heard God's voice. "The creative voice of God I heard resounding as *Aum*, the vibration of the Cosmic Motor." (20: p.143) Later on Yogananda confirmed that the spiritual experiences were bestowed upon the disciples only after he was totally prepared for it. "A master bestows the divine experience of cosmic consciousness when his disciple, by meditation, has strengthened his mind to a degree where the vast vistas would not overwhelm him. Mere intellectual

willingness or open-mindedness is not enough. Only adequate enlargement of consciousness by yoga practice and devotional *bhakti* can prepare one to absorb the liberating shock of omnipresent." He added to it, "The Lord as the Cosmic Vision is drawn by that magnetic ardour into the seeker's range of consciousness." (20: p.145)

4. The social environment rampant during Buddha's times was implicit with the brahminic tradition and legacies. It perpetuated the traditional cosmological beliefs in which there always existed a supreme God whose grace was necessary to reach the final goal in life. Buddhism has not been constructed on those principles. It is rather rooted in the absence of any single authoritarian belief or word relating to God. The truth is that it is derived from the firmly held Buddhist belief that 'man's mind is the creative centre of his universe and it has infinite capacity for change and growth. Therefore, belief in any cosmological laws or epistemological and theological positions would never be relevant to the Buddhist point of view. Sri Yogananda's quest for self-realisation proceeds on a path that has already been discovered by several spiritual masters before him. It is a sure path which has a security extended by a supernatural power to its devotees. Thus, there lies a sort of dependence in its quest for the final discovery.

Buddha holds an entirely different viewpoint in that respect. For him, reaching the realms of total awareness depends primarily on one's mind. After attaining awakening, he comes to the conclusion that 'the mind possesses endless capacity for change and growth'. This discovery provides a very positive message to man. Buddha's procedure is purely pragmatic too. Anyone, who sincerely and resolutely walks on the path proposed by him, can reach the realms of enlightenment.

The Unparalleled Faith

The truth is that Buddhism is not a specific dogma set up to counter to other dogmas. Instead, it is a path which the historic Buddha walked on. It is also possible for any sincere human being to walk on it. This kind of walk on a path is open to all accounts, for one of Buddha's often used titles is *Tathagata* that means as noted before, 'one who has come and gone this way'.

Buddha certainly emphasised that 'man is the instrument of his own destiny'. This very thought sets Buddhism apart from other faiths of the world. Buddha in his last speech before leaving this world spoke to his disciples, "Work out your own salvation with diligence. Be lamps unto yourselves." Such rulings of the departing Buddha, consisting of strong psychological emphasis on man as the means of his own freedom, have at times led to indicate Buddhism simply as a humanistic or even atheistic philosophy of faith, in which there is no place for any supernatural entity. Buddha did not construct the Ultimate Reality in line with any divine authority. As a result, he always kept silence whenever someone asked questions relating to God's existence or possibility of the existence of hell or heaven. He also did not argue about the existence of a soul. He always kept quiet on such issues or diverted the attention of the questioning person.

Buddha is not really seen as a saviour but only as an awakened person who discovers the universal truth to which he spends almost forty-five years of his precious life. The best part of his preaching lies in indicating that 'man must walk on the Way, which is a progressive way to develop oneself mentally, morally spiritually and physically as well'. It is also the basic structure on which the Mahayana* branch of Buddhism has built its own forms of discipline and instructions. Perhaps there is no other faith in the world other than Buddhism which has emphasised that man's future entirely depends on his own mental makeup. It is frequently projected in the *Dhammapada* in which his tenets, contained in the form of verses, are seen as the preparation for curing human misery, sickness and egocentrism. In that respect, Buddha's findings are unparalleled.

Burma's most respected shrine, the golden stupa of the Shwedagon in Rangoon. Rising to over 320 feet, the Shwedagon is reported to house eight of Buddha's hairs.

---

* Buddhism later on developed into two different branches known as the Hinayana and the Mahayana. The Hinayana means 'the Lesser Vessel or vehicle'. The Mahayana denotes the 'Greater Vehicle of Salvation'. Late on a new term, Theravada or 'The Way of the Elders' came into practice, which is now considered a more acceptable designation than Hinayana.

CHAPTER FIVE

Last Visit to Kapilavastu

When Channa returned from the forest carrying the prince's garments and other finery, mourning dawned in the palace. Kapilavastu was no longer a place of festivity. The entire subject of the state was also shocked to learn that the prince had abandoned home for good. They all felt as if something very precious was lost. Consequently, they remembered him and mourned all the time. Most people in Kapilavastu were greatly dismayed to learn about his unusual decision to become a recluse. The prince Siddhartha was extremely precious to all of them as not only he looked captivating, he was also a very kind person. He possessed an extremely compassionate demeanour and never tried to hurt anyone. He always kindled compassion and love towards all whom he met and whom he knew by chance. Although he was not permitted to keep in regular touch with the public on account of his father's apprehensions that he might become an ascetic if he happened to witness unhappiness, still all loved him dearly. When the stories of his kind disposition tracked through the courtiers' mouth to the general public, they learnt all about him. They adored him for his courage, sportsmanship, and other human qualities. Now all was finished. Their prince and in whom they hoped to be a very successful future king, had departed from them for good. All were shocked to learn that Siddhartha had left home because he was in search of the cause of human suffering.

As time passed and news about Siddhartha's persistent efforts to find solution for his problem did not reach Kapilavastu regularly, people gradually calmed down. Now they did not mourn for him but they were surely concerned for his safety and well-being. But the centre of mourning was still Siddhartha's family. None of them could forget him for a moment since when he had left. The king missed him to a great extent for he too loved him too much. Yashodhara constantly wept for him. She was extremely unhappy, more so because of Rahul who was so young when he left them. She always loved Siddhartha so intimately that she could not immediately believe that he would leave them without waking them up. When she learnt that the reason for his deserting them was related to the good of the people, she was overwhelmed with emotions and reverence. She immediately put off her ornaments and abandoned all the royal comforts. The newly born child, Rahul, grew up gradually knowing very little about his father. All he learnt about him from the people, who loved him dearly, often disturbed him greatly. The more he learnt about him, the more eagerly he desired to see him.

The ancient Indian tradition holds that when a person renounces the world, he is supposed to die for his past and is never expected to go back home. Whatever news tracked down to Kapilavastu about him, was not enough to keep Yashodhara happy. Therefore she mourned for him persistently without any hope to see him in future. In the meantime, Rahul grew as a tall and a fine lad. He looked much after him and was loved by his people like his father. Whenever some news about Siddhartha came to the palace from far and wide, the parents and Yashodhara thanked God to learn that he was at least alive and was keeping on well. Thus, almost seven years passed without much change in their doleful environment.

One day all of a sudden, a maid came running to Yashodhara and told her that she had some unusual news about a Buddha who was known to be an awakened one. He was staying in the forest near their town with a great following of men. The maid also added that the awakened man taught *dharma* with an open heart in a way that none had so far taught. She finally said that it was also a great rumour that the man who taught *dharma* was none other than the prince Siddhartha. When the king Shuddhodhana learnt that his lost son was staying not far from their town, he was filled with joy. But he was also angry for Siddhartha had left him without any notice. The king loved him so much that he had provided him every kind of comfort he required when he was the prince. Even if he required his kingdom he would have not hesitated to give it up for him. Why did he leave everything all of a sudden? This thought disturbed the king Shuddhodhana constantly.

As soon as Shuddhodhana learnt that Siddhartha had been camping with his monks not far away from Kapilavastu, he decided to see him at once. Torn between love and anger, the king mounted on his royal horse and departed for the forest. When the king reached the place where Buddha had been staying for a couple of days, he asked one of the monks to see his son at once. When Buddha learnt that his father had come to see him, he instantly left his hermitage to welcome him. Even during those days, the Indian tradition for the children to welcome and greet their parents by kneeling before them and touching their feet, was rampant. The king Shuddhodhana also expected Siddhartha to kneel before his father. But before it was done, the king found himself kneeling down before his son, as his extraordinary radiance impelled him to do so inadvertently. Buddha, reflecting a great reverence for his father, made him rise by holding him with both the hands.

When the king looked at his son who was then attired as a recluse, his heart was filled with sorrow. He wanted to see him a great king in life. Instead he became an ascetic. After a pause for a moment, when he controlled his emotions, he started hurling angry questions. He demanded of him to answer the questions that had been bothering him for so long. The king then asked him why he had abandoned all of them without any reason when every kind of comfort was showered upon him. After silence for a moment, he again asked him why he did leave them all when they loved him so dearly. Buddha listened to his father's angry questions patiently and stood in front of him quietly until he calmed down. When the king had no more questions to ask and seemed to have cooled down, Buddha looked at him very compassionately and replied politely. He said to the king that if he had accepted to rule his father's kingdom, he would have ruled over only a small kingdom. But after he had become a recluse, his kingdom was extended to the limitless lands as his love was boundless and extended to the whole world. Then he added that he had brought with him some unusual tidings which were priceless and would provide the king certain guaranties to safeguard him against death and darkness. His message was also implicit with a promise to show him the way that would lead him beyond sorrow for ever.

When the king listened to Buddha's words, his remaining anguish was totally subsided and he felt completely satisfied. After staying in his son's company for a while, he returned to his palace with a clear and a calm mind which had no disturbing questions any more. Rather he was wondering at Buddha's words and was eager to know what kind of message his son had for him with which all his sorrows would finally depart. When he reached the palace with his retinue, first he met Yashodhara who had been eagerly waiting for the last seven years to hear something from an eye witness about her lost husband. The king after a brief talk with his daughter-in-law retired to his chamber.

Visiting Yashodhara

The next morning the king awoke to hear the sound of some kind of uproar that came from the street down. Similarly Yashodhara also awoke to hear those sounds in the street below. Some of her maids, who had also heard the sound of that uproar, came running to her. They informed her that probably someone, who possessed a divinely radiance, was coming towards the palace with a great following of people. He looked like a god. They also implored her to come to the balcony and witness herself the spectacular scene that moved with the radiant person. The maids also concluded that the brilliant looking man was none other than the prince Siddhartha who was now bearing saffron robes only. Listening to the maids, Yashodhara rushed to the balcony to witness that unusual scene. The moment she recognised her man, she called Rahul to perceive all what she was observing from her balcony. Then she asked him to go down into the street and meet the radiant looking person who was obviously his father. She also implored Rahul to pay him adequate regards and love. Instantly Rahul disappeared down the street. Yashodhara and her maids watched him reaching Buddha after pushing his way through the crowd. When Rahul reached right in front of Buddha, he touched his feet with complete reverence, and then stood straight before him. Looking straight into his father's eyes, he asked him firmly, why he had left him in his mother's care alone when he was hardly a few months old.

Rahul's candid expression was so full of dismay that it could have moved any hard-hearted person. The Blessed One, obviously with great care and love, lifted him into his arms. Then he glanced at him with a compassionate look and slowly removed the external royal robe from his body. In its place, he covered him with a saffron robe that indicated that he was accepted to be as one of his youngest disciples. Rahul was only seven years old when he was ordained to the Order. Records display that he was the only child who was allowed to become Buddha's disciple. When all that was happening, the king Shuddhodhana also reached the street to meet his son. Yashodhara and her maids were watching that extraordinary scene from the top and were wondering what would happen next. When the father and the son met again, they exchanged their mutual love and respect. Then the king invited Buddha to come to the palace to meet other people who had been waiting to see him.

Unbounded Love

While all that was happening, the maids were constantly imploring Yashodhara to go down and to see her man. They told her that even though he had become a recluse and there was no place for a woman in his life, he would surely like to see her. But Yashodhara did not respond to her maids' requests. She told them that she would wait for him in her palace with the hope that he would certainly come to see her for she possessed boundless love for him. Listening to Yashodhara's reply, the maids kept quiet. In the meantime, they heard the sound of some footsteps that were approaching towards their mistress' chamber. After a few moments, they heard someone knocking at the door. When the maids opened the door they saw the king Shuddhodhana followed by Buddha standing just behind the king outside the door. As soon as Yashodhara looked at her husband standing behind the king, she took a few steps forward and fell on his knees, sobbing bitterly. It was quite a doleful sight which made the king also cry silently. When Buddha lifted her on her feet, she repeatedly asked him why he had left her when she worshipped him like a god and loved him more than her own life.

It was at this moment that the king came forward and told Buddha that from the time Channa brought back his robes and royal jewellery, Yashodhara also put away her finery. Since that day she had been mourning. When she learnt that he slept on the floor in the forests, she too stopped sleeping on her bed. Instead she took a simple mat to sleep over in the night. When the news came that he was eating only once during the day, she too ate only once in a day. After listening to her loving conduct, Buddha's heart must have filled with great compassion for her. He looked at her with great affection and told her in a most polite manner that her days of crying were over now. What she needed was to start a new life in which her love would not be limited to one person but would be showered to all the humanity. He also told her that he would teach her the way that would deliver her from her personal sorrows and help her learn to love the entire humanity. When Yashodhara listened to Buddha, she gradually calmed down and looked at the Blessed One with great respect. She also showed her eagerness to learn all what he had to teach her to go beyond her sorrow.

Quits Kapilavastu for Good

After a short time, Buddha left the palace and came back to his abode situated in the nearby forest. As long as he stayed there, people came to see him from Kapilavastu and nearby towns to seek his blessings. He too had great time there as many of the people who visited him, belonged to the king Shuddhodhana's court and were his former servants and attendants. A great number of these male folk sought his permission to join the Order.

His father was also one of them who after getting his approval became a member of his monistic order. But so far there were no women to be ordained to that Order. It is reported that some of his dearest women like Yashodhara, his aunts and his foster mother who tried to seek his permission to become members of his *sangha*, were refused by him. Buddha was an extremely wise person. He knew it well that if men and women lived together there could be problems of personal nature. He believed that the women should live at home and observe the rules implicit in the *dharma* prescribed by him. He also stated that if they followed the Eightfold Path and other precepts, they would certainly reach beyond the limits of misery. He suggested strongly that if the women relinquished their cravings and selfish fulfilments, they would surely reach the domain of *nirvana*.

It is really difficult to ascertain the timings of the parables and the tales that are connected to Buddha's magnificent life. Many of his tales are so impressive and exemplary that one can take advantage of them any time during one's life and get redeemed. I, therefore, present here one of his parables that can help us, if we earnestly understand the purpose behind and pursue the principle implicit in it.

Perhaps one of the visitors, who came to see him when he had camped near Kapilavastu, made a queer enquiry. He asked the Blessed One, "What do you get from meditation?" Buddha gazed at the person confidently and told him that he did not get anything from it. The enquiring man looked at him with a perplexed expression and asked him again that if meditation did not provide him anything, of what use was it. After listening to the man's further query, Buddha told him that on the contrary he had lost many things through meditation. After a short while, Buddha continued that through meditation, he lost anger, sickness, apprehensions that rise during old age, and fear of loneliness as well as of death. He lost all that on account of meditation. Ultimately meditation led him to *nirvana*. Such intelligent discourses brought great awakening among the ignorant people and provided them enough insight to fight against their selfish cravings.

Thus, after staying for several days in the forest around Kapilavastu, Buddha, accompanied with the monks and his other followers, left for another town. Although no kind of craving was left within him after he had attained enlightenment, yet he must have felt relieved of certain burdens if they were lying dormant in his subconscious after visiting Kapilavastu. He knew it well that there was no fault of Yashodhara and Rahul when he left them unaware in the middle of the night. Perhaps that kind of heavy feeling must have lurked in the heart of the Compassionate One. It was probably the reason that soon after he attained enlightenment, he decided to visit his hometown to see them all. When both, the king Shuddhodhana and Yashodhara, poured their emotions in front of him, Buddha must have felt relieved of his hidden pain too. Though no one talked about all such things, but all looked happier after meeting one another.

When Buddha refused Yashodhara and the other ladies permission to enter the Order, Yashodhara did not feel satisfied. Consequently, she along with Siddhartha's foster mother, decided to follow him. As soon as Buddha left Kapilavastu, Yashodhara, after seeking permission from the elders, also left home with the other lady. They travelled on foot for a number of days. Finally they caught him up near Vaishali, which was two hundred miles away from Kapilavastu. When they reached Vaishali, they decided to rest for a while that night. They thought that the next day when they recovered from the fatigue of the journey, they would approach Buddha once again with a greater vigour and better reasoning.

Legends indicate that when the ladies reached Vaishali, Ananda happened to see them first. Ananda was one of the few disciples of Buddha who loved him dearly. Perhaps he was the only one who also attended to all his personal requirements. He immediately understood the purpose of the ladies' visit to Vaishali. He also knew that Buddha had already refused to accept them. Considering the nature of the problem, he really did not know exactly what to do under such circumstances. Then after contemplating for a while and collecting enough courage, he decided to approach the Blessed One, hoping that he being a compassionate person would concede to his request. When Ananda reached inside his hermitage, he did not say a word. Instead he stood in silence in front of him. As Buddha looked at him, he felt that Ananda had something in his mind. After a pause for a moment, he asked Ananda rather in a concerned tone, whether he had something in his mind to ask him. Encouraged by the Master's affectionate query which certainly reflected his concern as well, Ananda decided to tell him all what he had in his mind. Ananda was also one of his brilliant disciples. He, therefore, knew it well how to present his case and persuade his Master to agree to his request. Bearing a humble demeanour, he looked into his Master's eyes and stated politely that he had a difficult question and he was not able to find an answer to it. The Blessed One asked him instantly to state his question.

Ananda, placing his question before Buddha, enquired, "Is it men only who are able to conquer their suffering?"

Buddha said to him with great affection, "All human beings are capable to overcome suffering."

Then Ananda put another question and asked him, "Is it only man who can renounce his selfish cravings and attain *nirvana*?"

Buddha repeated once again that every human being had the capacity to renounce the selfish cravings and attain *nirvana.*

Buddha's reply was quite encouraging to Ananda. Listening to it, he enquired of him humbly, "If that is the case, then why only men are allowed to join the *sangha*?"

The Blessed One smiled and told him that he had understood his intentions implicit in the discussion. Then he said to him that both men and women, who earnestly desired to renounce their personal cravings and relinquished their selfish fulfilment, had equal right to be admitted to his Order. From that time onwards, women were also admitted to Buddha's Order. Thus, Yashodhara and the foster mother were the first two ladies who became the first nuns of Buddha's *sangha.* It also gave birth to the two branches of the *sangha* that became world's foremost monastic community.

CHAPTER SIX

Entering Nirvana for the Last Time

The Impending Demise

For almost forty-five years, Buddha preached the *dharma* for the benefit of all those who desired to seek the path. Thousands of listeners and devotees attended his discourse sessions and clarified their doubts during those illuminating meetings. Ultimately time came when signs of weakening of his body started appearing apparently. By then he had reached the eightieth year of his age. During the past forty-five years when he preached rigorously, he tried very hard to keep himself fit. Yet regular travelling and lack of rest at times had secretly taken its toll. As a result, he fell seriously ill in his eightieth year. Buddha fought hard to dispel his physical pain and fever that lasted for many days. It was this time that Ananda and his other close disciples feared that he might die. Finally Buddha recovered from that illness and almost got back his normal strength. But he was in his eightieth year now and it was quite normal not to possess the same physical strength and agility that he used to have in the past. It, therefore, became natural for some of his followers to consider how the *sangha* would function in the absence of the inspiring Buddha.

The *sangha* was established with great care and efforts of the Blessed One. So the monks thought that it was opportune time to consider the details about how it would function when Buddha was gone. Devdutta, one of Buddha's cousins who had joined the Order shortly after it was established, suggested that a successor needed to be chosen before Buddha finally departed. He also suggested that he, being the cousin of the Blessed One, was the right person for that position. Buddha heard all that patiently and then said to all who were present that the *sangha* would govern itself and no new leader was needed to be chosen after his death. He then suggested that all decisions regarding the functioning of the *sangha* would stay in the hands of the simple majority of the monks present at that time. He added that the *sangha* would work as a democratic institution and would not function on hierarchical basis.

Buddha also emphasised that the monks were required to be self-reliant in his absence. What they required was to work hard in line with their conscience. He also added that he strongly believed that the *sangha* would never fail without his guidance so he did not need to leave any instructions regarding how to make it function in his absence. He said, "Why should I leave any instructions? Be a refuge unto yourselves, Ananda." He then added, "Rely on yourselves and nothing else. Hold fast to the *dharma* as your lamp, hold fast to the *dharma* as your refuge, and you shall surely reach *nirvana*." Then the monks, who had assembled to listen to Buddha's final verdict regarding how to administer the *sangha,* left him to resume their respective duties. Before they left, Buddha summoned Ananda and told him to ask the monks to assemble at Vaishali on the following day.

When the monks gathered at Vaishali on the next day, Buddha urged them to follow the Eightfold Path earnestly with diligence so that their example would help them and others to run the *sangha* smoothly. At the same time, it should also become exemplary to others to follow it for centuries. After Buddha finished talking to the monks, he called Ananda and asked him to sit by him. Then he confided in him and said solemnly that Mara had once again appeared before him second time. It was an indication that he had to leave this world. Listening to Buddha's sombre words, Ananda's heart was filled with extreme dolefulness.

On the next day Buddha left Vaishali with his disciples for a nearby place known as Kusinara. Though Buddha was totally recovered from his former illness, it had left its marks on him. His body was growing weaker day by day. On the way to Kusinara, he asked Ananda to stop for a while to rest in a mango grove near a small town known as Pava. The grove belonged to one of his followers named Cunda who was delighted to receive Buddha and his disciples. He served them with sumptuous food which he offered with great affection. It is reported that one of the dishes offered by Cunda was rotten. It gave Buddha food poisoning. The old age and recent illness had already debilitated his body. He was hardly able to withstand this sudden attack on his weak constitution. He struggled hard to sustain his health through that food poisoning. After a while, Buddha felt repeated pain in his body, but he asked his disciples to continue on their journey.

It is reported that hardly he had travelled a short distance from Cunda's place that he felt very weak and desired to rest again for a while. He asked Ananda to spread his robe under a shady tree where he could rest for some time. When he was resting under the tree a stranger happened to see him. Impressed by Buddha's extraordinary appearance, he brought him a new robe, which Ananda helped him to wear. Whenever Buddha rested for a while and felt that he was better, he resumed his journey.

Later on the same day they arrived at the town Kusinara. All decided to stay there for the night. Buddha also felt extremely tired and asked Ananda to make a bed for him. He prepared a bed for him in a grove of *sal* trees. There Buddha laid down in the lion posture, holding the weight of his body on the right side on one hand supporting his head. One can still witness him in that posture in some of his statues. One such statue representing Buddha's last posture can be seen in Thailand where there are still so many followers of Buddha.

Entering into Parinirvana

Like any other spiritual ascetic Buddha also knew it that what day and time he would leave this world finally. Vivekananda, his guru Sri Ram Krishna and Paramahansa Yogananda, all knew ahead about their final release from the mortal body. Therefore, knowing it well that the time of his final release had come, he asked Ananda to go into the town of Kusinara and tell people that he would shed his body after the midnight. So those who desired to see him for the last time could come to see him. He also asked Ananda to go to Cunda to tell him that he should never feel guilty of serving him unwholesome food and blame himself for causing his demise. It was to happen that way so he should never feel accountable for it. It is reported that as soon as the people learnt about Buddha's final departure from this world, they came in great numbers to see him. At times the number of visiting people was so big that it became very difficult for Ananda to control them from overcrowding his chamber.

As Buddha was finally lying down on his right side with one leg resting on the other, he looked completely mindful and serene. His dear disciple, Ananda, standing near him could not bear him passing away right in front of him. Although Buddha looked self-possessed and tranquil, it was certain that he would soon die. At that moment, Ananda could not resist himself and burst out in agony, crying bitterly. Buddha, despite of his physical ailment and severe pain in his body, kept serene and gently reminded Ananda of the basic truth that all who were born would certainly die one day. Then he briefly addressed his disciples for the last time. First he asked them if anyone had any doubt about the Way he had suggested. None uttered a word and all remained silent for some time. Buddha reflecting a look of great satisfaction told them that they must never doubt about the teaching implicit in *dharma* propounded by him. He advised them not to mourn after he was gone. Finally Buddha entered into deep meditation and entered into *Parinirvana*. Just like him, later on not far from our times, Vivekananda and Paramahansa Yogananda also entered into deep *samadhi* (meditation) a little before their death. The moments of Buddha's death are probably most remarkably stated in the legendary scripture, the *Sutta Nipata*. It says:

> *As the flame blown out by the wind*
> *Goes to rest and cannot be defined*
> *So the wise man freed from individuality*
> *Goes to rest and cannot be defined.*

Buddha finally left all of us. During forty-five years of his teaching of *dharma* he attracted hundreds of thousands of disciples. The Order he had started successfully, gradually established itself over the centuries. His principles expanded throughout India and to the west in the nearby countries. During the reign of the great Indian king Ashoka, in the third century BC, it also moved southwards until it reached Sri Lanka. The king Ashoka sent his emissaries to distant lands to spread Buddhism. Later on during another Indian Emperor known as Kaniska, who ruled Kushan people during the first century BC and who controlled a big territory that extended up to what is now the Soviet Union, the Buddhism was accepted by most of the people. Under Kaniska's patronage, the spread of Buddhism was on its peak and enjoyed its golden age. Historians report that during Kaniska and his successors' period, Buddhism was accepted by the people from the Gandhara region to the east of Khyber Pass (currently northern Pakistan). Gradually, it was taken from the Central Asia to the land of China. At the same time, it was also introduced to the regions now known as Burma and Thailand. From China, it entered into the thresholds of Korea and then later on reached Japan.

Perhaps all that expansion of Buddhism could happen as Buddha was able to influence a great number of people by his pragmatic and realistic teaching. He influenced numberless people who willingly accepted his *dharma*. They became his ardent disciples and travelled far and wide to spread his message to the people. Despite Buddha's inability to explain very closely what his exact experience had been during attainment of enlightenment, it was his remarkable charismatic personality that won the hearts of people who came to see him and to listen to his message. His disciples, who went to distant lands as his religious ambassadors to spread his message far and wide, were totally intoxicated and influenced by his radiant and unusual individuality. They constantly worked hard without caring for difficult conditions and unwelcoming circumstances that they faced during their long or short journey.

Incredible Contribution

It seems imperative to reflect upon the nature and extent of Buddha's unusual contribution to the humanity before closing this small work. After his demise, the *sangha* worked very successfully for a couple of centuries. Then there came upheavals that hampered its normal growth to a large extent. But Buddhism has survived even after two thousand five hundred years after its birth. What is that in his teaching that it has survived all the atrocities of the tyrants during the past few centuries and currently it is becoming popular once again, mostly in foreign lands? In view of that it seems essential to make an assessment of all what Buddha contributed to the humanity. Besides his promise to redeem us all from our suffering, there are certain valuable characteristics that are implicit in his teaching. That probably makes it one of the best faiths in the world. If we follow religiously the *dharma* proposed by him, we find that it contains hundreds of precepts which if followed seriously, can easily redeem a human being whether living as a householder or as a recluse. Let us examine the issues that have placed Buddhism at the forefront of the world religions while assessing Buddha's contribution as a great thinker and a spiritual person.

Six to seven years back, when I came closer to the Buddhist literature and went through some of his parables, I felt extremely delighted and attracted towards it. When the pace of my attention grew further towards the precepts interwoven with the parables, I felt that his teaching is extremely rich in providing knowledge that can help humans in directing their actions to a safer road that would surely lead them to the realms of peace and happiness. For example, the first line of the verse contained in the *Dhammapada*, tells us: "We become what we think." How true it is that we become in life exactly what we think for us to become. Things of that nature influenced me a lot. I reckon similar things are largely instrumental in bringing a great number of people every year very close to Buddhism.

Six Aspects of Religion

"How someone, known as Buddha or the Enlightened, was created in this world?" is a question that needs to be answered by re-examining the religious circumstances rampant in India during the time Buddha was born in 563 BC. In fact, to understand Buddha's contribution in the right perspective, we would need to find out the existing picture of Hinduism that to a large extent triggered it to happen. Philip Novak suggests that there are six aspects of religion that need to be examined before assessing Buddha's contribution. These are: authority, ritual, speculation, tradition, grace and finally mystery. During Buddha's times, these six aspects of the existing religion, i.e. Hinduism, had fettered human life with the belief that without active involvement in all those aspects of religion no being can reach the end of the road to redemption. That means one had to accept the authority of the Brahmins who held the reigns of religion in their hands. Rituals became means to obtain unprecedented results. Both speculation and tradition believed to have experiential bases and were considered meaningful. Likewise God's grace and mystery were also considered important to comprehend the Infinite.

These six issues related to religion in Buddha's days were degenerated to a large extent. The authority of the Brahmins had become totally hereditary. They had started exploiting the people and held the religious secrets more for their own benefit rather than for the general public. Likewise rituals became just mechanical to obtain any astounding results. Tradition had become totally outdated and speculation had no experimental base left to convince people. Besides, Sanskrit in which most religious teaching was done by the Brahmins was no longer spoken or understood by majority of the people. God's grace was often misunderstood by the people as the Brahmins always tried to mould it as they desired. The theory of *karma* was gradually taken to be confusing and ended with the belief in fatalism. Above all, an environment of confusion lay rampant among the people, for corrupt practices had polluted the entire religious environment of the country. It was Buddha who stood against all such outdated practices and blind-beliefs. As a result of his scientific approach towards the human problems, his word gradually became important and popular. (15: p.22-24)

When Buddha started teaching his religious or philosophical precepts, Hinduism had already started getting setbacks. Mahavir Swami, a contemporary of Buddha and one of the important pillars of the Jain religion, had also started attacking it against its corrupt practices. When Buddha came on the scene, his message appealed the people to a great extent for the Way he had suggested was not only simple but could also be tested by the individual himself. Besides, Buddha did not teach a religion that was based on any authority. He not only condemned the authority of the Brahmins, but also tried to make everything public regarding his own concept of religion. Whatever he discovered about the procedure relating human redemption, he placed it before the people as such and did not keep any secrets from them. It easily won people's confidence in him. Even on his deathbed, he assured the people that he had not kept anything back from them.

More than condemning the authority of the Brahmins, he invoked the individual person to test all what had been said by the tradition or stated in the sacred books and indicated through the rituals. He insisted that every individual must test the religious ideas before accepting them and making them part of the life. He emphasised to accept the ideas only when they proved to be good to one's life and to condemn them when they were harmful. With this kind of thought he, in fact, insisted that all must possess self-reliance in relation to the religious practices and must never take things for granted if they had been handed over to them from the past.

Buddha repeatedly condemned practising rites or rituals. He criticised them for being full of superstitions leading nowhere. "There was no truth in seeking peace, happiness or redemption through the practices that were backed by mere superstition," he said emphatically. He considered rituals as simply trappings and irrelevant, for they worked like fetters to human freedom and led to conditioning. Once if conditioning took place, it would never let anyone attain liberation from the blind belief, which in itself was a great barrier to salvation. He not only condemned involvement in the traditional rituals but also insisted that no such rituals should be developed by the monks while practising the Way he had suggested them. He repeatedly indicated that his entire procedure was based on logic and his personal discovery and was purely pragmatic. He emphatically insisted that the monks should never involve in any kind of temptation or speculation while practising his procedure. If they did so, it would lead to the same age old methodology and practices which would ultimately give way to superstition in their minds.

His teaching was far from speculation as he always insisted on evidence and personal discovery. In order to avoid confusion and to dispel superstition, he always avoided answering questions such as 'whether the world is eternal or not eternal, whether it is finite or not finite, whether the soul and the body are the same or whether they are two separate entities, or whether Buddha would exist after death or he would not'. His conspicuous silence on these issues made many of his disciples unhappy, for they wanted answers to these questions. They often wondered 'why the Blessed One kept a long silence when such issues were brought to discussion'. Buddha's silence was not meaningless. He kept silence on these issues, for he thought that such enquiries would lead to fruitless speculation which had no real basis. On the contrary, his practice-programme was exacting and realistic. He never wanted his disciples to wander in quandary and abandon the hard road to practise the right Path he had suggested.

Buddha always persuaded his monks and followers to stay free from the burdens of the blind-beliefs that people often carried in their minds on account of conditioning created by the practice of rituals and beliefs generated by tradition. With this, he added one more dimension to his teaching. It was that he gave his message in the vernacular in which most people communicated and which they understood well. The Brahmins still used Sanskrit to communicate the religious precepts to the people. During Buddha's time, the use of Sanskrit had become limited. It was no longer the language of the common person. When Buddha communicated his precepts in the language which could be understood by most of the people, not only his message became clear to them, but they were also greatly fascinated by it.

It was the time when most people had taken for granted that the chain of birth and rebirth would never end and go on for thousands of years. During every incarnation people would go on suffering on account of their past *karma* which would never change even if they pass through innumerable births and rebirths. It was also believed that they could never take birth in a higher class like that of the Brahmins. Such ideas based on fatalism had created a kind of great dissatisfaction and unending distress among the people. Such beliefs filled their lives with no hopes for a better life after death.

Buddha was totally against this kind of prevailing fatalism. He rejected all such thoughts vehemently and provided a great hope to the people that they could attain peace and salvation even during their present life. He said, "Here is a path to the end of suffering." If one wanted to get redeemed and desired to change the course of one's life, one simply required to walk on it keeping a strong resolution and initiative. He insisted that no god or gods were required to provide man the required peace or salvation. It was man himself who required walking on the Path to reach the goal. He thus condemned the notion that only Brahmins could attain or provide enlightenment. He told the people that one's caste had noting to do with the attainment of *nirvana*. Whatever one's caste be, one could always make it in this very lifetime. He implored people to come to him and listen carefully what he stated. If they honestly followed the Path he had suggested, they would surely realise their goal, which they could easily test for themselves.

Buddha never believed in the forecasts and soothsaying as he condemned supernatural intervention. He thought that the belief in forecasts was a sort of holding in low-arts. Although he discerned from his own experience during attainment of enlightenment that human mind was capable of powers that could enact miracles, he warned his monks not to perform any miracles. To use their power for performing miracles could lead them to make shortcuts in their efforts which would easily divert them from hard and practical work he had suggested to attain the goal. Buddha perceived danger in that kind of pursuits for it would cultivate superstitions and blind beliefs. So he warned the monks to keep away from involving in any sorts of acts that could lead them to cultivate superstition.

Positive Contribution

Buddha kept silence on the issue of God's existence and any supernatural entity. He condemned superstitions, mystery, tradition and rituals while practising religion. As long as he lived, he never permitted such issues to enter the domain of his religion or thought-process. But many such things did track into the Buddhist practices later on. Keeping all that aside right now, let us briefly discover what was his positive contribution for the benefit of the people. In a nutshell, his teaching was **empirical and it had scientific appeal.** It was also pragmatic. It was definitely of **remedial nature** too. First he discovered the cause of human suffering and then he suggested a way to end that suffering. His teaching was also **psychological as it appealed to human mind directly.** He started with the human suffering, sought its solution and provided ways to cope up with it. **His way to help the people was liberal.** Although initially he accepted men to be his followers, but later on he admitted women too to become nuns and stay in the *sangha.* **He totally rejected the caste system and candidly declared that every kind of person whether belonging to a high caste or a low caste could reach the domain of salvation** provided the Path he had suggested was followed religiously.

So far most appeals made by the traditional religion were directed to the masses, but Buddha **especially made his appeal to the individuals.** Little before his death, he advised Ananda to be 'a lamp unto himself and not to take refuge in any external entity'. He insisted that man should hold fast to the Truth and discover his own freedom with hard work coupled with wisdom. In the *Dhammapada*, he often invokes the wise to stick to the right path. He holds that 'only those who are wise reach the other shore and leave the darkness behind and follow the light*'. Perhaps Buddha was a pioneer in discovering the endless power of human mind. He said that the mind possessed a series of thought-movements as unconnected as an ongoing movie. 'The mind is the thoughts, and only the speed of thinking creates the illusion that there is something continuous and substantial. It is that illusion which leads to form a personal ego which seems so real and seeks satisfaction in fulfilling various cravings which are the main cause of human suffering.' (4: p.60)

It was his most appealing discovery to the people at that time as most people were quite unaware of such lucid explanations. Buddha not only explored the depths of the mind, but also provided highly convincing and acceptable answers to the difficult questions which were never positively answered by the religious traders of his time. His appeal made to the individuals carried a positive note and was pragmatic to a great extent, for one who desired to walk on the road indicated by him could test it himself. Nothing could be true than that and the Truth is always appealing and convincing even to the less wise people.

---

* *Dhammapada*, Chapter on 'The Wise'

Index

C

D

E

N

O

P

Q

R

S

T

U

V

W

Y

The Bibliography

The Path of Dharma

1. Allen Charles, (2002), **The Search for Buddha**, New York: Carroll & Publishers
2. Chang, Garma C.C., (1971), **The Buddhist Teaching of Totality**, University Park, Pa., and London: The Pennsylvania State University Press
3. Cleary Thomas, (1995), **The Dhammapada**, New York: Bantam Books
4. Easwaran Eknath, (1985), **The Dhammapada**, California: Nilgiri Press
5. Duane O.B., (1997), **Zen Buddhism**, London: Brockhamption Press
6. Kornfield Jack, (1993), **Teachings Of Buddha**, Boston: Shambhala
7. Mascaro Juan, (1973), **The Dhammapada**, London: Penguin Books
8. Mason Cora,(1953), **Socrates, The Man Who Dared To Ask**, Boston: Beacon Press
9. Powell Andrew, (1989), **Living Buddhism**, New York: Harmony Books
10. Prasoon Shrikant, (2007), **Knowing Buddha**, New Delhi: Pustak Mahal

11. Reps Paul & Senzaki, (1994), **Zen Flesh, Zen Bones, Boston: Shambhala**

12. Ross Nancy Wilson, (1981), **Buddhism: A way of Life and Thought**, New York: Vintage Books

13. Sharma A.P., (2000), **Concept of Freedom**, I Universe, On Line Publishers, USA

14. Sharma A.P., (2004), **Seeking Right Mindfulness**, Ahmedabad: Law Publishers

15. Smith Houston & Novak Philip, (2003), **Buddhism**, San Francisco: Harper

16. Sturat Holroyd, (1980), **The Quest Of The Quiet Mind**, Wellinborough (England): Aquarian Press

17. The Dalai Lama & Carriere Jean-Claude, (1996), **Violence & Compassion**, New York: Doubleday

18. Titmuss Christopher, (2000), **An Awakened Life**, Boston: Sambhala

19. Vadanya, (1990), **Introducing Buddhism**, New York: Barnes & Noble Books

20. Yogananda Paramahansa, (1946), **Autobiography of a Yogi**, Los Angeles: Self-Realization Fellowship

Knowing Guru Nanak

Life and Teachings

—Prof. Shrikant Prasoon

The grace and wisdom that Guru Nanak got from the Ek Omkar, he showered on and shared with 'all'.

Have we collected our share, stored and used it to be wise and graceful?

If yes, then know its value and effects; if not, then regain through 'Knowing Guru Nanak', the essence of the Essential Guru to live fully and correctly the life of a human being and to get "Bliss, Beatitude and Salvation."

'Knowing Guru Nanak' paints the Gurus, presents their teachings, shows the overlooked obvious, helps in flowing in the mainstream, gives vision and wisdom of the Guru and opens ajar the tightly closed conscience, widens the view and keeps awakened, active and conscious like the Guru.

Size: 5.5" x 8.5" • Pages: 200
Price: Rs. 96/- • Postage: Rs. 15/-